The Art of Public Speaking

The Art of Public Speaking

Dale Carnegie

Ocean Books Pvt. Ltd.
ISO 9001:2015 Publishers

Published by
Ocean Books (P) Ltd.
4/19 Asaf Ali Road,
New Delhi-110 002 (INDIA)
e-mail: info@oceanbooks.in

ISBN 978-81-8430-261-5
THE ART OF PUBLIC SPEAKING
by Dale Carnegie

Edition
2025

Price
₹ 350.00 (Rupees Three Hundred Fifty only)

Printed at
Narula Printers, Delhi

A Foreword

The efficiency of a book is like that of a man, in one important respect: its attitude towards its subject is the first source of its power. A book may bc full of good ideas well expressed, but if its writer views his subject from the wrong angles even his excellent advice may prove to be ineffective.

Training in public speaking is not a matter of externals, primarily; it is not a matter of imitation, fundamentally; it is not a matter of conformity to standards, at all. Public speaking is public utterance, public issuance, of the man himself; therefore the first thing both in time and in importance is that the man should be and think and feel things that are worthy of being given forth. Unless there be something of value within, no tricks of training can ever make of the talker anything more than a machine, albeit a highly perfected machine, for the delivery of other men's goods. So self-development is fundamental in our plan.

The second principle lies close to the first: The man must enthrone his will to rule over his thought, his feelings, and all his physical powers, so that the outer self may give perfect, unhampered expression to the inner. It is futile, to lay down systems of rules for voice culture, intonation, gesture, and what not, unless these two principles of having something to say and making the will sovereign have at least begun to make themselves felt in the life.

The third principle will, we surmise, arouse no dispute: No one can learn *how* to speak who does not first speak as best he can. That may seem like a vicious circle in statement, but it will bear examination.

Many teachers have begun with the *how* Vain effort! It is an ancient truism that we learn to do by doing. The first thing for the beginner in public speaking is to speak, not to study voice and gesture and the rest. Once he has spoken he can improve himself by self-observation or according to the criticisms of those who hear.

But how shall he be able to criticise himself? Simply by finding out three things: What are the qualities which by common consent go to make up an effective speaker; by what means at least some of these qualities may be acquired; and what wrong habits of speech in himself work against his acquiring and using the qualities which he finds to be good.

Experience, then, is not only the best teacher, but the first and the last. But experience must be a dual thing, the experience of others must be used to supplement, correct and justify our own experience; in this way we shall become our own best critics only after we have trained ourselves in self-knowledge, the knowledge of what other minds think, and in the ability to judge ourselves by the standards we have come to believe are right. "If I ought," said Kant, "I can."

An examination of the contents of this volume will show how consistently these articles of faith have been declared, expounded, and illustrated. The student is urged to begin to speak at once of what he knows. Then he is given simple suggestions for self-control, with gradually increasing emphasis upon the power of the inner man over the outer. Next, the way to the rich storehouses of material is pointed out. And finally, all the while he is urged to speak, *speak*, *SPEAK* as he is applying to his own methods, in his own *personal* way, the principles he has gathered from his own experience and observation and the recorded experiences of others.

—**J. BERG ESENWEIN**

The Art of Public Speaking

Sense never fails to give them that have it, Words enough to make them understood. It too often happens in some conversations, as in Apothecary Shops, that those Pots that are Empty, or have Things of small Value in them, are as gaudily Dress'd as those that are full of precious Drugs.

They that soar too high, often fall hard, making a low and level Dwelling preferable. The tallest Trees are most in the Power of the Winds, and Ambitious Men of the Blasts of Fortune. Buildings have need of a good Foundation, that lie so much exposed to the Weather.

—WILLIAM PENN

Contents

	A Foreword	5
	The Art of Public Speaking	7
1.	Acquiring Confidence Before an Audience	11
2.	The Sin of Monotony	17
3.	Efficiency through Emphasis and Subordination	21
4.	Efficiency through Change of Pitch	27
5.	Efficiency through Change of Pace	32
6.	Pause and Power	37
7.	Efficiency through Inflection	45
8.	Concentration in Delivery	49
9.	Force	53
10.	Feeling and Enthusiasm	61
11.	Fluency through Preparation	67
12.	The Voice	72
13.	Voice Charm	80
14.	Distinctness and Precision of Utterance	90
15.	The Truth about Gesture	95
16.	Methods of Delivery	104

17. Thought and Reserve Power 113
18. Subject and Preparation 122
19. Influencing by Exposition 134
20. Influencing by Description 144
21. Influencing by Narration 158
22. Influencing by Suggestion 169
23. Influencing by Argument 182
24. Influencing by Persuasion 187
25. Influencing the Crowd 194
26. Riding the Winged Horse 200
27. Growing a Vocabulary 209
28. Memory Training 217
29. Right Thinking and Personality 226
30. After-dinner and other Occasional Speaking 231
31. Making Conversation Effective 234

1

Acquiring Confidence Before an Audience

There is a strange sensation often experienced in the presence of an audience. It may proceed from the gaze of the many eyes that turn upon the speaker, especially if he permits himself to steadily return that gaze. Most speakers have been conscious of this in a nameless thrill, a real something, pervading the atmosphere, tangible, evanescent, indescribable. All writers have borne testimony to the power of a speaker's eye in impressing an audience. This influence which we are now considering is the reverse of that picture, the power their eyes may exert upon him, especially before he begins to speak: after the inward fires of oratory are fanned into flame the eyes of the audience lose all terror.

William Pittenger, Extempore Speech—

Students of public speaking continually ask, "How can I overcome self-consciousness and the fear that paralyses me before an audience?"

Did you ever notice while looking from a train window that some horses feed near the track and never even pause to look up at the thundering carriage, while just ahead at the next railway crossing a farmer's wife will be nervously trying to quiet her scared horse as the train goes by?

How would you cure a horse that is afraid of cars, graze him in a back-woods lot where he would never see steam-engines or automobiles, or drive or pasture him where he would frequently see the machines?

Apply horse-sense to ridding yourself of self-consciousness and fear: face an audience as frequently as you can, and you will soon stop shying. You can never attain freedom from stage-fright by reading a treatise. A book may give you excellent suggestions on how best to conduct yourself in the water, but sooner or later you must get wet, perhaps even strangle and be "half scared to death." There are a great many "wetless" bathing suits worn at the seashore, but no one ever learns to swim in them. To plunge is the only way.

Practice, practice, PRACTICE in speaking before an audience will tend to remove all fear of audiences, just as practise in swimming will lead to confidence and facility in the water. You must learn to speak by speaking.

Do not be disheartened if at first you suffer from stage-fright. For one reason or another, some master-speakers never entirely overcome stage-fright, but it will pay you to spare no pains to conquer it.

Be Absorbed by Your Subject

Blacksmiths sometimes twist a rope tight around the nose of a horse, and by thus inflicting a little pain they distract his attention from the shoeing process. One way to get air out of a glass is to pour in water. Apply the blacksmith's homely principle when you are speaking. If you feel deeply about your subject you will be able to think of little else. Concentration is a process of distraction from less important matters. It is too late to think about the cut of your coat once you are upon the platform, so centre your interest on what you are about to say, fill your mind with your speech-material and, like the infilling water in the glass, it will drive out your unsubstantial fears.

Self-consciousness is undue consciousness of self, and, for

the purpose of delivery, self is secondary to your subject, not only in the opinion of the audience, but, if you are wise, in your own. It is sheer egotism to fill your mind with thoughts of self when a greater thing is there, *TRUTH* Say this to yourself sternly, and shame your self-consciousness into quiescence. If the theater caught fire you could rush to the stage and shout directions to the audience without any self-consciousness, for the importance of what you were saying would drive all fear-thoughts out of your mind.

Far worse than self-consciousness through fear of doing poorly is self-consciousness through assumption of doing well. The first sign of greatness is when a man does not attempt to look and act great. Before you can call yourself a man at all, Kipling assures us, you must "not look too good nor talk too wise." Nothing advertises itself so thoroughly as conceit.

Have Something to Say

The trouble with many speakers is that they go before an audience with their minds a blank. It is no wonder that Nature, abhorring a vacuum, fills them with the nearest thing handy, which generally happens to be, "I wonder if I am doing this right! How does my hair look? I know I shall fail." Their prophetic souls are sure to be right.

It is not enough to be absorbed by your subject, to acquire self-confidence you must have something in which to be confident. If you go before an audience without any preparation, or previous knowledge of your subject, you ought to be self-conscious, you ought to be ashamed to steal the time of your audience. Prepare yourself. Know what you are going to talk about, and, in general, how you are going to say it. Have the first few sentences worked out completely so that you may not be troubled in the beginning to find words. Know your subject better than your listeners know it, and you have nothing to fear.

After Preparing for Success, Expect It

Let your bearing be modestly confident, but most of all be modestly confident within. Over-confidence is bad, but to tolerate premonitions of failure is worse, for a bold man may win attention by his very bearing, while a rabbit-hearted coward invites disaster.

Humility is not the personal discount that we must offer in the presence of others, against this old interpretation there has been a most healthy modern reaction. Any man who thoroughly knows himself must feel True humility but it is not a humility that assumes a worm like meekness; it is rather a strong, vibrant prayer for greater power for service, a prayer that Uriah Heep could never have uttered.

Washington Irving once introduced Charles Dickens at a dinner given in the latter's honour. In the middle of his speech Irving hesitated, became embarrassed, and sat down awkwardly. Turning to a friend beside him he remarked, "There, I told you I would fail, and I did."

If you believe you will fail, there is no hope for you. You will.

Rid yourself of this I-am-a-poor-worm-in-the-dust idea. You are a god, with infinite capabilities. "All things are ready if the mind be so." The eagle looks the cloudless sun in the face.

Assume Mastery Over Your Audience

In public speech, as in electricity, there is a positive and a negative force. Either you or your audience are going to possess the positive factor. If you assume it, you can almost invariably make it yours. If you assume the negative, you are sure to be negative. Assuming a virtue or a vice vitalises it. Summon all your power of self-direction, and remember that though your audience is infinitely more important than you are, the truth is more important than both of you, because it is eternal. If your mind falters in its leadership, the sword will drop from your hands. Your assumption of being able to instruct or lead or inspire a multitude or even a small group of people may appal you as being colossal impudence, as indeed it may be; but having once essayed to speak, be courageous. *BE* courageous, it lies within you to be what you will. *MAKE* yourself be calm and confident.

In facing your audience, pause a moment and look them over, a hundred chances to one they want you to succeed, for what man is so foolish as to spend his time, perhaps his money, in the hope that you will waste his investment by talking dully?

Concluding Hints

Do not make haste to begin, haste shows lack of control.

Do not apologise. It ought not to be necessary; and if it is, it will not help. Go straight ahead.

Take a deep breath, relax, and begin in a quiet conversational tone as though you were speaking to one large friend. You will not find it half so bad as you imagined; really, it is like taking a cold plunge: after you are in, the water is fine. In fact, having spoken a few times you will even anticipate the plunge with exhilaration. To stand before an audience and make them think your thoughts after you is one of the greatest pleasures you can ever know.

So cast out fear, for fear is cowardly, when it is not mastered. The bravest know fear, but they do not yield to it. Face your audience pluckily, if your knees quake, *MAKE* them stop. In your audience lies some victory for you and the cause you represent. Go win it. The world owes its progress to the men who have dared, and you must dare to speak the effective word that is in your heart to speak, for often it requires courage to utter a single sentence. But remember that men erect no monuments and weave no laurels for those who fear to do what they can.

Is all this unsympathetic ?

Man, what you need is not sympathy, but a push. No one

doubts that temperament and nerves and illness and even praiseworthy modesty may, singly or combined, cause the speaker's cheek to blanch before an audience, but neither can any one doubt that coddling will magnify this weakness. The victory lies in a fearless frame of mind. Prof. Walter Dill Scott says: "Success or failure in business is caused more by mental attitude even than by mental capacity." Banish the fear attitude; acquire the confident attitude. And remember that the only way to acquire it is, to *acquire* it.

In this foundation chapter we have tried to strike the tone of much that is to follow. Many of these ideas will be amplified and enforced in a more specific way; but through all these chapters on an art which Mr. Gladstone believed to be more powerful than the public press, the note of justifiable self-confidence must sound again and again.

□

2

The Sin of Monotony

One day Ennui was born from Uniformity.
—MOTTE

Our English has changed with the years so that many words now connote more than they did originally. This is true of the word *monotonous*. From "having but one tone," it has come to mean more broadly, "lack of variation."

The monotonous speaker not only drones along in the same volume and pitch of tone but uses always the same emphasis, the same speed, the same thoughts, or dispenses with thought altogether.

Monotony, the cardinal and most common sin of the public speaker, is not a transgression, it is rather a sin of omission.

To tell you that your speech is monotonous may mean very little to you, so let us look at the nature, and the curse, of monotony in other spheres of life, then we shall appreciate more fully how it will blight an otherwise good speech.

If the record player in the adjoining apartment grinds out just three selections over and over again, it is pretty safe to assume that your neighbour has no other records. If a speaker uses only a few of his powers, it points very plainly to the fact that the rest of his powers are not developed. Monotony reveals our limitations.

In its effect on its victim, monotony is actually deadly, it will drive the bloom from the cheek and the lustre from the eye as quickly as sin, and often leads to viciousness. The worst punishment that human ingenuity has ever been able to invent is extreme monotony, solitary confinement. Lay a marble on the table and do nothing eighteen hours of the day but change that marble from one point to another and back again, and you will go insane if you continue long enough.

So this thing that shortens life, and is used as the cruelest of punishments in our prisons, is the thing that will destroy all the life and force of a speech. Avoid it as you would shun a deadly dull bore. The "idle rich" can have half-a-dozen homes, command all the varieties of foods gathered from the four corners of the earth, and sail for Africa or Alaska at their pleasure; but the poverty-stricken man must walk or take a street car, he does not have the choice of yacht, Car, or special train. He must spend the most of his life in labour and be content with the staples of the food-market. Monotony is poverty, whether in speech or in life. Strive to increase the variety of your speech as the business man labours to augment his wealth.

Bird-songs, forest glens, and mountains are not monotonous, it is the long rows of brown-stone fronts and the miles of paved streets that are so terribly same. Nature in her wealth gives us endless variety; man with his limitations is often monotonous. Get back to Nature in your methods of speech-making.

The power of variety lies in its pleasure-giving quality. The great truths of the world have often been couched in fascinating stories, "Less Miserables," for instance. If you wish to teach or influence men, you must please them, first or last. Strike the same note on the piano over and over again. This will give you some idea of the displeasing, jarring effect monotony has on the ear. The dictionary defines "monotonous" as being synonymous with "wearisome." That is putting it mildly. It is maddening.

How to Conquer Monotony

We obviate monotony in dress by replenishing our wardrobes. We avoid monotony in speech by multiplying our powers of speech. We multiply our powers of speech by increasing our tools.

The carpenter has special implements with which to construct the several parts of a building. The organist has certain keys and stops which he manipulates to produce his harmonies and effects. In like manner the speaker has certain instruments and tools at his command by which he builds his argument, plays on the feelings, and guides the beliefs of his audience. To give you a conception of these instruments, and practical help in learning to use them, is the purpose of the immediately following chapters.

Many speakers still use ox-cart methods in their speech instead of employing automobile or overland-express methods. They are ignorant of laws that make for efficiency in speaking. Just to the extent that you regard and use the laws that we are about to examine and learn how to use will you have efficiency and force in your speaking; and just to the extent that you disregard them will your speaking be feeble and ineffective. We cannot impress too thoroughly upon you the necessity for a real working mastery of these principles. They are the very foundations of successful speaking. "Get your principles right," said Napoleon, "and the rest is a matter of detail."

It is useless to shoe a dead horse, and all the sound principles in the world will never make a live speech out of a dead one. So let it be understood that public speaking is not a matter of mastering a few dead rules; the most important law of public speech is the necessity for truth, force, feeling, and life. Forget all else, but not this.

When you have mastered the mechanics of speech outlined in the next few chapters you will no longer be troubled with monotony. The complete knowledge of these principles and the ability to apply them will give you great variety in your powers of expression. But they cannot be mastered and applied by thinking or reading about them, you must practise, practise, *PRACTISE*. If no one else will listen to you, listen to yourself, you must always be your own best critic, and the severest one of all.

The technical principles that we lay down in the following chapters are not arbitrary creations of our own. They are all founded on the practices that good speakers and actors adopt, either naturally and unconsciously or under instruction, in getting their effects.

It is useless to warn the student that he must be natural. To be natural may be to be monotonous. The little strawberry up in the Arctics with a few tiny seeds and an acid tang is a natural berry, but it is not to be compared with the improved variety that we enjoy here. The dwarfed tree on the rocky hillside is natural, but a poor thing compared with the beautiful tree found in the rich, moist bottom lands. Be natural, but improve your natural gifts until you have approached the ideal, for we must strive after idealised nature, in fruit, tree, and speech.

□

3

Efficiency through Emphasis and Subordination

In a word, the principle of emphasis...is followed best, not by remembering particular rules, but by being full of a particular feeling.
—**C.S. BALDWIN**, *Writing and Speaking*

The gun that scatters too much does not bag the birds. The same principle applies to speech. The speaker that fires his force and emphasis at random into a sentence will not get results. Not every word is of special importance, therefore only certain words demand emphasis.

You say Massa *CHU* setts and Minne APolis, you do not emphasize each syllable alike, but hit the accented syllable with force and hurry over the unimportant ones. Now why do you not apply this principle in speaking a sentence? To some extent you do, in ordinary speech; but do you in public discourse? It is there that monotony caused by lack of emphasis is so painfully apparent.

So far as emphasis is concerned, you may consider the average sentence as just one big word, with the important word as the accented syllable. Note the following:

"Destiny is not a matter of chance. It is a matter of choice."

You might as well say *MASS-A-CHU-SETTS*, emphasizing every syllable equally, as to lay equal stress on each word in the foregoing sentences.

Speak it aloud and see. Of course you will want to emphasize *destiny*, for it is the principal idea in your declaration, and you will put some emphasis on not, else your listeners may think you are affirming that destiny is a matter of chance. By all means you must emphasize chance, for it is one of the two big ideas in the statement.

Another reason why *chance* takes emphasis is that it is contrasted with *choice* in the next sentence. Obviously, the author has contrasted these ideas purposely, so that they might be more emphatic, and here we see that contrast is one of the very first devices to gain emphasis.

As a public speaker you can assist this emphasis of contrast with your voice. If you say, "My horse is not *black*," what color immediately comes into mind? White, naturally, for that is the opposite of black. If you wish to bring out the thought that destiny is a matter of choice, you can do so more effectively by first saying that *"DESTINY* is *NOT* a matter of *CHANCE."* Is not the colour of the horse impressed upon us more emphatically when you say, "My horse is *NOT BLACK*. He is *WHITE* " than it would be by hearing you assert merely that your horse is white?

In the second sentence of the statement there is only one important word, *choice*. It is the one word that positively defines the quality of the subject being discussed, and the author of those lines desired to bring it out emphatically, as he has shown by contrasting it with another idea. These lines, then, would read like this:

"DESTINY is *NOT* a matter of *CHANCE*. It is a matter of CHOICE" Now read this over, striking the words in capitals with a great deal of force.

In almost every sentence there are a few *MOUNTAIN PEAK WORDS* that represent the big, important ideas. When you pick up the evening paper, you can tell at a glance which are the important news articles. Thanks to the editor, he does not tell about a "hold up" in Hong Kong in the same sized type as he uses to report the death of five firemen in your home city. Size of type is his device to show emphasis in bold relief. He brings out sometimes even in red headlines the striking news of the day.

It would be a boon to speech-making if speakers would conserve the attention of their audiences in the same way and emphasize only the words representing the important ideas. The average speaker will deliver the foregoing line on destiny with about the same amount of emphasis on each word. Instead of saying, "It is a matter of *CHOICE*," he will deliver it, "It is a matter of choice," or *"IT IS A MATTER OF CHOICE"*, both equally bad.

Charles Dana, the famous editor of *The New York Sun*, told one of his reporters that if he went up the street and saw a dog bite a man, to pay no attention to it. *The Sun* could not afford to waste the time and attention of its readers on such unimportant happenings. "But," said Mr. Dana, "if you see a man bite a dog, hurry back to the office and write the story." Of course that is news; that is unusual.

Now the speaker who says *"IT IS A MATTER OF CHOICE"* is putting too much emphasis upon things that are of no more importance to metropolitan readers than a dog bite, and when he fails to emphasize "choice" he is like the reporter who "passes up" the man's biting a dog. The ideal speaker makes his big words stand out like mountain peaks; his unimportant words are submerged like stream-beds. His big thoughts stand like huge oaks; his ideas of no especial value are merely like the grass around the tree.

From all this we may deduce this important principle: *EMPHASIS* is a matter of *CONTRAST* and *COMPARISON*.

Note the following editorial, printed in the same type as given here.

We do not know what the President THOUGHT when he got that message, or what the elephant thinks when he sees the mouse, but we do know what the President DID.

The words *THOUGHT* and *DID* immediately catch the reader's attention because they are different from the others, not especially because they are larger. If all the rest of the words in this sentence were made ten times as large as they are, and *DID* and *THOUGHT* were kept at their present size, they would still be emphatic, because different.

Take the following from Robert Chambers' novel, "The Business of Life." The words *you, had, would,* are all emphatic, because they have been made different.

He looked at her in angry astonishment.

"Well, what do *you* call it if it isn't cowardice, to slink off and marry a defenceless girl like that!"

"Did you expect me to give you a chance to destroy me and poison Jacqueline's mind? If I *had* been guilty of the thing with which you charge me, what I have done *would* have been cowardly. Otherwise, it is justified."

To make a word emphatic, deliver it differently from the manner in which the words surrounding it are delivered. If you have been talking loudly, utter the emphatic word in a concentrated whisper, and you have intense emphasis. If you have been going fast, go very slow on the emphatic word. If you have been talking on a low pitch, jump to a high one on the emphatic word. If you have been talking on a high pitch, take a low one on your emphatic ideas. Read the chapters on "Inflection," "Feeling," "Pause," "Change of Pitch," "Change of Tempo." Each of these will explain in detail how to get emphasis through the use of a certain principle.

In this chapter, however, we are considering only one form of emphasis: that of applying force to the important word and subordinating the unimportant words. Do not forget: this is one of the main methods that you must continually employ in getting your effects.

Let us not confound loudness with emphasis. To yell is not a sign of earnestness, intelligence, or feeling. The kind of force that we want applied to the emphatic word is not entirely physical. True, the emphatic word may be spoken more loudly, or it may be spoken more softly, but the *real* quality desired is intensity, earnestness. It must come from within, outwards.

A speaker said: "The curse of this country is not a lack of education. It's politics." He emphasized *curse, lack, education, politics*. The other words were hurried over and thus given no comparative importance at all. The word *politics* was flamed out with great feeling as he slapped his hands together indignantly. His emphasis was both correct and powerful. He concentrated all our attention on the words that meant something, instead of holding it up on such words as *of this, a, of, It's*.

What would you think of a guide who agreed to show New York to a stranger and then took up his time by visiting Chinese laundries and boot-blacking "Parlours" on the side streets? There is only one excuse for a speaker's asking the attention of his audience: He must have either truth or entertainment for them. If he wearies their attention with trifles they will have neither vivacity nor desire left when he reaches words of importance. You do not dwell on these small words in your everyday conversation, because you are not a conversational bore. Apply the correct method of everyday speech to the platform. As we have noted elsewhere, public speaking is very much like conversation enlarged.

Sometimes, for big emphasis, it is advisable to lay stress on every single syllable in a word, as *absolutely* in the following sentence:

"I absolutely refuse to grant your demand".

Now and then this principle should be applied to an emphatic sentence by stressing each word. It is a good device for exciting special attention, and it furnishes a pleasing variety. Patrick Henry's notable climax could be delivered in that manner very effectively:

Strongly emphasizing a single word has a tendency to suggest its antithesis. Notice how the meaning changes by merely putting the emphasis on different words in the following sentence. The parenthetical expressions would really not be needed to supplement the emphatic words.

I intended to buy a house this Spring (even if you did not). I *INTENDED* to buy a house this Spring (but something prevented).

I intended to *BUY* a house this Spring (instead of renting as heretofore).

I intended to buy a *HOUSE* this Spring (and not an automobile).

I intended to buy a house *THIS* Spring (instead of next Spring).

I intended to buy a house this *SPRING* (instead of in the Autumn).

When a great battle is reported in the papers, they do not keep emphasizing the same facts over and over again. They try to get new information, or a "new slant." The news that takes an important place in the morning edition will be relegated to a small space in the late afternoon edition. We are interested in new ideas and new facts. This principle has a very important bearing in determining your emphasis. Do not emphasize the same idea over and over again unless you desire to lay extra stress on it.

You must understand that there are no steel-riveted rules of emphasis. It is not always possible to designate which word must, and which must not be emphasized. One speaker will put one interpretation on a speech, another speaker will use different emphasis to bring out a different interpretation. No one can say that one interpretation is right and the other wrong. This principle must be borne in mind.

□

4

Efficiency through Change of Pitch

> Speech is simply a modified form of singing: the principal difference being in the fact that in singing the vowel sounds are prolonged and the intervals are short, whereas in speech the words are uttered in what may be called "staccato" tones, the vowels not being specially prolonged and the intervals between the words being more distinct. The fact that in singing we have a larger range of tones does not properly distinguish it from ordinary speech. In speech we have likewise a variation of tones, and even in ordinary conversation there is a difference of from three to six semi-tones, as I have found in my investigations, and in some persons the range is as high as one octave.
>
> —**WILLIAM SCHEPPEGRELL,**
> *Popular Science Monthly*

By pitch, as everyone knows, we mean the relative position of a vocal tone, as, high, medium, low, or any variation between. In public speech we apply it not only to a single utterance, as an exclamation or a monosyllable (*Oh! or the*) but to any group of syllables, words, and even sentences that may be spoken in a single tone. It is important to keep this distinction in mind, for the efficient speaker not only changes the pitch of successive syllables (see Chapter 7, "Efficiency through Inflection"), but gives a different pitch to different parts, or word-groups, of successive sentences. It is this phase of the subject which we are considering in this chapter.

Every Change in the Thought Demands a Change in the Voice-Pitch

Whether the speaker follows the rule consciously, unconsciously, or subconsciously, this is the logical basis upon which all good voice variation is made, yet this law is violated more often than any other by *public* speakers. A criminal may disregard a law of the state without detection and punishment, but the speaker who violates this regulation suffers its penalty at once in his loss of effectiveness, while his innocent listeners must endure the monotony, for monotony is not only a sin of the perpetrator, as we have shown, but a plague on the victims as well.

Change of pitch is a stumbling block for almost all beginners, and for many experienced speakers also. This is especially true when the words of the speech have been memorised.

If you wish to hear how pitch-monotony sounds, strike the same note on the piano over and over again. You have in your speaking voice a range of pitch from high to low, with a great many shades between the extremes. With all these notes available, there is no excuse for offending the ears and taste of your audience by continually using the one note. True, the reiteration of the same tone in music, as in pedal point on an organ composition, may be made the foundation of beauty, for the harmony weaving about that one basic tone produces a consistent, insistent quality not felt in pure variety of chord sequences. In like manner the intoning voice in a ritual may, though it rarely does, possess a solemn beauty. But the public speaker should shun the monotone as he would a pestilence.

Continual Change of Pitch is Nature's Highest Method

In our search for the principles of efficiency we must continually go back to Nature. Listen, really listen, to the birds sing. Which of these feathered tribes are most pleasing in their vocal efforts: those whose voices, though sweet, have little or no range, or those that, like the canary, the lark, and the nightingale, not only possess a considerable range but utter their notes in continual variety of combinations? Even a sweet-toned chirp, when reiterated without change, may grow maddening to the enforced listener.

The little child seldom speaks in a monotonous pitch. Observe the conversations of little folk that you hear on the street or in the home, and note the continual changes of pitch. The unconscious speech of most adults is likewise full of pleasing variations.

Imagine someone speaking the following, and consider if the effect would not be just about as indicated. Remember, we are now not discussing the inflection of single words, but the general pitch in which phrases are spoken.

(High pitch) "I'd like to leave for my vacation tomorrow (lower) still, I have so much to do. (Higher) Yet I suppose if I wait until I have time I'll never go."

Repeat this, first in the pitches indicated, and then all in the one pitch, as many speakers would. Observe the difference in naturalness of effect.

Anonymous

The necessity for changing pitch is so self-evident that it should be grasped and applied immediately. However, it requires patient drill to free yourself from monotony of pitch.

In natural conversation you think of an idea first, and then find words to express it. In memorised speeches you are liable to speak the words, and then think what they mean, and many speakers seem to trouble very little even about that. Is it any wonder that reversing the process should reverse the result? Get back to Nature in your methods of expression.

Read the following selection in a nonchalant manner, never pausing to think what the words really mean. Try it again, carefully studying the thought you have assimilated. Believe the idea, desire to express it effectively, and imagine an audience before you. Look them earnestly in the face and repeat this truth. If you follow directions, you will note that you have made many changes of pitch after several readings.

"It is not work that kills men; it is worry. Work is healthy; you can hardly put more upon a man than he can bear. Worry is rust upon the blade. It is not the revolution that destroys the machinery but the friction."

—**HENRY WARD BEECHER**

Change of Pitch Produces Emphasis

This is a highly important statement. Variety in pitch maintains the listener's interest, but one of the surest ways to compel attention, to secure unusual emphasis, is to change the pitch of your voice suddenly and in a marked degree. A great contrast always arouses attention. White shows whiter against black; a cannon roars louder in the Sahara silence than in the Chicago hurly burly, these are simple illustrations of the power of contrast.

"What is Congress going to do next?
(High pitch) |
|
| I do not know."
(Low pitch)

By such sudden change of pitch during a speech the speaker achieved great emphasis and suggested the gravity of the question he had raised.

The foregoing order of pitch-change might be reversed

with equally good effect, though with a slight change in seriousness, either method produces emphasis when used intelligently, that is, with a common-sense appreciation of the sort of emphasis to be attained.

In attempting these contrasts of pitch it is important to avoid unpleasant extremes. Most speakers pitch their voices too high. Shakespeare said that a soft, gentle, low voice was "an excellent thing in woman;" it is no less so in man, for a voice need not be blatant to be powerful,, and *must* not be, to be pleasing.

In closing, let us emphasize anew the importance of using variety of pitch. You sing up and down the scale, first touching one note and then another above or below it. Do likewise in speaking.

Thought and individual taste must generally be your guide as to where to use a low, a moderate, or a high pitch.

□

5

Efficiency through Change of Pace

Hear how he clears the points o' Faith Wi' rattlin' an' thumpin'! Now meekly calm, now wild in wrath, He's stampin' an' he's jumpin'.

—**ROBERT BURNS**, *Holy Fair*

The Latins have bequeathed to us a word that has no precise equivalent in our tongue, therefore we have accepted it, body unchanged, it is the word *tempo*, and means *rate of movement*, as measured by the time consumed in executing that movement.

Thus far its use has been largely limited to the vocal and musical arts, but it would not be surprising to hear tempo applied to more concrete matters, for it perfectly illustrates the real meaning of the word to say that an ox-cart moves in slow tempo, an express train in a fast tempo. Our guns that fire six hundred times a minute, shoot at a fast tempo; the old muzzle loader that required three minutes to load, shot at a slow tempo. Every musician understands this principle: it requires longer to sing a half note than it does an eighth note.

Now tempo is a tremendously important element in good platform work, for when a speaker delivers a whole address at very nearly the same rate of speed he is depriving himself of one of his chief means of emphasis and power. The baseball pitcher, the bowler in cricket, the tennis server, all know the value of change of pace, change of tempo, in delivering their ball, and so must the public speaker observe its power.

Change of Tempo Lends Naturalness to the Delivery

Naturalness, or at least seeming naturalness, as was explained in the chapter on "Monotony," is greatly to be desired, and a continual change of tempo will go a long way towards establishing it. Change of pace is one of the most effective tools of the actor. While it must be admitted that the stilted mouthings of many actors indicate cloudy mirrors, still the public speaker would do well to study the actor's use of tempo.

There is, however, a more fundamental and effective source at which to study naturalness, a trait which, once lost, is shy of recapture: that source is the common conversation of any well-bred circle. *This* is the standard we strive to reach on both stage and platform, with certain differences, of course, which will appear as we go on. If speaker and actor were to reproduce with absolute fidelity every variation of utterance, every whisper, grunt, pause, silence, and explosion, of conversation as we find it typically in everyday life, much of the interest would leave the public utterance. Naturalness in public address is something more than faithful reproduction of Nature, it is the reproduction of those *typical* parts of Nature's work which are truly representative of the whole.

The realistic story-writer understands this in writing dialogue, and we must take it into account in seeking for naturalness through change of tempo.

Suppose you speak the first of the following sentences in a slow tempo, the second quickly, observing how natural the effect is. Then speak both with the same rapidity and note the difference.

> "I can't recall what I did with my knife. Oh, now I remember I gave it to Mary."

We see here that a change of tempo often occurs in the same sentence, for tempo applies not only to single words, groups of words, and groups of sentences, but to the major parts of a public speech as well.

Change of Tempo Prevents Monotony

The canary in the cage before the window is adding to the beauty and charm of his singing by a continual change of tempo. If King Solomon had been an orator, he undoubtedly would have gathered wisdom from the song of the wild birds as well as from the bees. Imagine a song written with but quarter notes. Imagine a vehicle with only one speed.

Change of Tempo Produces Emphasis

Any big change of tempo is emphatic and will catch the attention. You may scarcely be conscious that a passenger train is moving when it is flying over the rails at ninety miles an hour, but if it slows down very suddenly to a ten-mile gait your attention will be drawn to it very decidedly. You may forget that you are listening to music as you dine, but let the orchestra either increase or diminish its tempo in a very marked degree and your attention will be arrested at once.

This same principle will procure emphasis in a speech. If you have a point that you want to bring home to your audience forcefully, make a sudden and great change of tempo, and they will be powerless to keep from paying attention to that point. These lines were spoken in a play:

"I don't want you to forget what I said. I want you to remember it the longest day you, I don't care if you've got six guns." The part up to the dash was delivered in a very slow tempo, the remainder was named out at lightning speed, as the character who was spoken to drew a revolver. The effect was so emphatic that the lines are remembered six months afterwards, while most of the play has faded from memory. The student who has powers of observation will see this principle applied by all our best actors in their efforts to get emphasis where emphasis is due. But remember that the emotion in the matter must warrant the intensity in the manner, or the effect will be ridiculous. Too many public speakers are impressive overnothing.

Thought rather than rules must govern you while practising change of pace. It is often a matter of no consequence which part of a sentence is spoken slowly and which is given in fast tempo. The main thing to be desired is the change itself.

Be careful in regulating your tempo not to get your movement too fast. This is a common fault with amateur speakers. Mrs. Siddons rule was, "Take time." A hundred years ago there was used in medical circles a preparation known as "the shot gun remedy;" it was a mixture of about fifty different ingredients, and was given to the patient in the hope that at least one of them would prove efficacious! That seems a rather poor scheme for medical practice, but it is good to use "shot gun" tempo for most speeches, as it gives a variety. Tempo, like diet, is best when mixed.

Practise the following selection, noting carefully where the tempo may be changed to advantage. Experiment, making numerous changes. Which one do you like best?

Dedication of Gettysburg Cemetery

Fourscore and seven years ago, our fathers brought forth upon this continent a new nation, conceived in liberty and dedicated to the proposition that all men are created equal. Now we are engaged in a great civil war, testing whether that nation, or any nation so conceived and so dedicated, can long endure.

We are met on a great battlefield of that war. We are met to dedicate a portion of it as the final resting-place of those who have given their lives that nation might live. It is altogether fitting and proper that we should do this.

But, in a larger sense, we cannot dedicate, we cannot

consecrate, we cannot hallow, this ground. The brave men, living and dead, who struggled here, have consecrated it, far above our power to add or to detract. The world will very little note nor long remember what we say here; but it can never forget what they did here.

It is for us, the living, rather, to be dedicated here to the unfinished work they have thus far so nobly carried on. It is rather for us to be here dedicated to the great task remaining before us: that from these honoured dead we take increased devotion to that cause for which they here gave the last full measure of devotion; that we here highly resolve that these dead shall not have died in vain; that the nation shall, under God, have a new birth of freedom, and that government of the people, by the people, for the people, shall not perish from the earth.

—ABRAHAM LINCOLN

□

6

Pause and Power

> The true business of the literary artist is to plait or weave his meaning, involving it around itself; so that each sentence, by successive phrases, shall first come into a kind of knot, and then, after a moment of suspended meaning, solve and clear itself.
>
> —GEORGE SAINTSBURY,
> on *English Prose Style, in Miscellaneous Essays.*

... pause ... has a distinctive value, expressed in silence; in other words, while the voice is waiting, the music of the movement is going on ... To manage it, with its delicacies and compensations, requires that same fineness of ear on which we must depend for all faultless prose rhythm. When there is no compensation, when the pause is inadvertent ... there is a sense of jolting and lack, as if some pin or fastening had fallen out.

— JOHN FRANKLIN GENUNG,
The Working Principles of Rhetoric.

Pause, in public speech, is not mere silence, it is silence made designedly eloquent.

When a man says: "I-uh-it is with profound-ah-pleasure

that-er-I have been permitted to speak to you tonight and-uh-uh-I should say-er", that is not pausing; that is stumbling. It is conceivable that a speaker may be effective in spite of stumbling, but never because of it.

On the other hand, one of the most important means of developing power in public speaking is to pause either before or after, or both before and after, an important word or phrase. No one who would be a forceful speaker can afford to neglect this principle, one of the most significant that has ever been inferred from listening to great orators. Study this potential device until you have absorbed and assimilated it.

It would seem that this principle of rhetorical pause ought to be easily grasped and applied, but a long experience in training both college men and maturer speakers has demonstrated that the device is no more readily understood by the average man when it is first explained to him than if it were spoken in *Hindoostani*. Perhaps this is because we do not eagerly devour the fruit of experience when it is impressively set before us on the platter of authority; we like to pluck fruit for ourselves, it not only tastes better, but we never forget that tree! Fortunately, this is no difficult task, in this instance, for the trees stand thick all about us.

One man is pleading the cause of another:

"This man, my friends, has made this wonderful sacrifice, for you and me."

Did not the pause surprisingly enhance the power of this statement? See how he gathered up reserve force and impressiveness to deliver the words "for you and me." Repeat this passage without making a pause. Did it lose in effectiveness?

Naturally enough, during a premeditated pause of this kind the mind of the speaker is concentrated on the thought to which he is about to give expression. He will not dare to allow his thoughts to wander for an instant, he will rather supremely centre his thought and his emotion upon the sacrifice whose service, sweetness and divinity he is enforcing by his appeal.

Concentration, then, is the big word here, no pause without it can perfectly hit the mark.

Efficient pausing accomplishes one or all of four results:

1. *Pause Enables the Mind of the Speaker to Gather His Forces Before Delivering the Final Volley*

It is often dangerous to rush into battle without pausing for preparation or waiting for recruits.

You can light a match by holding it beneath a lens and concentrating the sun's rays. You would not expect the match to flame if you jerked the lens back and forth quickly. Pause, and the lens gathers the heat. Your thoughts will not set fire to the minds of your listeners unless you pause to gather the force that comes by a second or two of concentration. Maple trees and gas wells are rarely tapped continually; when a stronger flow is wanted, a pause is made, Nature has time to gather her reserve forces, and when the tree or the well is reopened, a stronger flow is the result.

Use the same common sense with your mind. If you would make a thought particularly effective, pause just before its utterance, concentrate your mind-energies, and then give it expression with renewed vigour. Carlyle was right: "Speak not, I passionately entreat thee, till thy thought has silently matured itself. Out of silence comes thy strength. Speech is silvern, Silence is golden; Speech is human, Silence is divine."

Silence has been called the father of speech. It should be. Too many of our public speeches have no fathers. They ramble along without pause or break. Like Tennyson's brook, they run on forever. Listen to little children, the policeman on the corner, the family conversation around the table, and see how many pauses they naturally use, for they are unconscious of effects. When we get before an audience, we throw most of our natural methods of expression to the wind, and strive after artificial effects. Get back to the methods of Nature, and pause.

2. *Pause Prepares the Mind of the Audience to Receive Your Message*

Herbert Spencer said that Lentire the universe is in motion. So it is, and all perfect motion is rhythm. Part of rhythm is rest. Rest follows activity all through Nature. Instances: day and night; spring, summer, autumn, winter; a period of rest between breaths; an instant of complete rest between heart beats. Pause, and give the attention-powers of your audience a rest. What you say after such a silence will then have a great deal more effect.

When your country cousins come to town, the noise of a passing car will awaken them, though it seldom affects a seasoned city dweller. By the continual passing of cars his attention-power has become deadened. In one who visits the city but seldom, attention-value is insistent. To him the noise comes after a long pause; hence its power. To you, dweller in the city, there is no pause; hence the low attention-value. After riding on a train for several hours you will become so accustomed to its roar that it will lose its attention-value, unless the train should stop for a while and start again. If you attempt to listen to a clock-tick that is so far away that you can barely hear it, you will find that at times you are unable to distinguish it, but in a few moments the sound becomes distinct again. Your mind will pause for rest whether you desire it to do so or not.

The attention of your audience will act in quite the same way. Recognise this law and prepare for it, by pausing. Let it be repeated: the thought that follows a pause is much more dynamic than if no pause had occurred. What is said to you of a night will not have the same effect on your mind as if it had been uttered in the morning when your attention had been lately refreshed by the pause of sleep. We are told on the first page of the *Bible* that even the Creative Energy of God rested on the "seventh day." You may be sure, then, that the frail finite mind of your audience will likewise demand rest. Observe Nature, study her laws, and obey them in your speaking.

3. *Pause Creates Effective Suspense*

Suspense is responsible for a great share of our interest in life; it will be the same with your speech. A play or a novel is often robbed of much of its interest if you know the plot beforehand. We like to keep guessing as to the outcome. The ability to create suspense is part of woman's power to hold the other sex. The circus acrobat employs this principle when he fails purposely in several attempts to perform a feat, and then achieves it. Even the deliberate manner in which he arranges the preliminaries increases our expectation, we like to be kept waiting. We not only like to wait but we appreciate what we wait for. If fish bite too readily, the sport soon ceases to be a sport.

It is this same principle of suspense that holds you in a Sherlock Holmes story, you wait to see how the mystery is solved, and if it is solved too soon you throw down the tale unfinished. Wilkie Collins' formula for fiction writing well applies to public speech: "Make 'em laugh; make 'em weep; make 'em wait." Above all else make them wait; if they will not do that you may be sure they will neither laugh nor weep.

Thus pause is a valuable instrument in the hands of a trained speaker to arouse and maintain suspense. Willam Bryan said in a speech: "It was my privilege to hear", and he paused, while the audience wondered for a second who it was his privilege to hear, "the great evangelist", and he paused again; we knew a little more about the man he had heard, but still wondered to which evangelist he referred; and then he concluded: "Dwight L. Moody." Bryan paused slightly again and continued: "I came to regard him", here he paused again and held the audience in a brief moment of suspense as to how he had regarded Moody, then continued, "as the greatest preacher of his day." Let the dashes illustrate pauses and we have the following:

"It was my privilege to hear, the great evangelist, Dwight L. Moody., I came to regard him, as the greatest preacher of his day."

The unskilled speaker would have rattled this off with neither pause nor suspense, and the sentences would have fallen flat upon the audience. It is precisely the application of these small things that makes much of the difference between the successful and the unsuccessful speaker.

4. *Pausing After An Important Idea Gives it Time to Penetrate*

Any farmer will tell you that a rain that falls too fast will run off into the streams and do the crops but little good. A speech, like a rain, will not do anybody much good if it comes too fast to soak in. The farmer's wife follows this same principle in doing her washing when she puts the clothes in water, and pauses for several hours that the water may soak in. Why do we use this principle everywhere except in the communication of ideas? If you have given the audience a big idea, pause for a second or two and let them turn it over. See what effect it has. After the smoke clears away you may have to fire another 14-inch shell on the same subject before you demolish the citadel of error that you are trying to destroy. Take time. Don't let your speech resemble those tourists who try "to do" New York in a day. They spend fifteen minutes looking at the masterpieces in the Metropolitan Museum of Arts, ten minutes in the Museum of Natural History, take a peep into the Aquarium, hurry across the Brooklyn Bridge, rush up to the Zoo, and back by Grant's Tomb, and call that "Seeing New York." If you hasten by your important points without pausing, your audience will have just about as adequate an idea of what you have tried to convey.

Take time, you have just as much of it as our richest multimillionaire. Your audience will wait for you. It is a sign of smallness to hurry. The great redwood trees of California had burst through the soil five hundred years before Socrates drank his cup of hemlock poison, and are only in their prime today. Nature shames us with our petty haste. Silence is one of the most eloquent things in the world. Master it, and use it through pause.

* * * * *

In the following selections dashes have been inserted where pauses may be used effectively. Naturally, you may omit some of these and insert others without going wrong, one speaker would interpret a passage in one way, one in another; it is largely a matter of personal preference. A dozen great actors have played Hamlet well, and yet each has played the part differently. Which comes the nearest to perfection is a question of opinion. You will succeed best by daring to follow your own course, if you are individual enough to blaze an original trail.

"A moment's halt, a momentary taste of being from the well amid the waste, and lo! the phantom caravan has reached, the nothing it set out from, Oh make haste!

The worldly hope men set their hearts upon, turns ashes, or it prospers; and anon like snow upon the desert's dusty face, lighting a little hour or two, is gone.

The bird of time has but a little way to flutter, and the bird is on the wing."

You will note that the punctuation marks have nothing to do with the pausing. You may run by a period very quickly and make a long pause where there is no kind of punctuation. Thought is greater than punctuation. It must guide you in your pauses.

"A book of verses underneath the bough,, a jug of wine, a loaf of bread, and thou beside me singing in the wilderness, Oh, wilderness were paradise enow."

You must not confuse the pause for emphasis with the natural pauses that come through taking breath and phrasing. For example, note the pauses indicated in this selection from Byron:

"But *hush*!, *hark*!, that deep sound breaks in once more, And *nearer*!, *clearer*!, *deadlier* than before. *Arm*,

ARM!, it is, it is the cannon's opening roar!"

It is not necessary to dwell at length upon these obvious distinctions. You will observe that in natural conversation our words are gathered into clusters or phrases, and we often pause to take breath between them. So in public speech, breathe naturally and do not talk until you must gasp for breath; nor until the audience is equally winded.

A serious word of caution must here be uttered: do not overwork the pause. To do so will make your speech heavy and stilted. And do not think that pause can transmute commonplace thoughts into great and dignified utterance. A grand manner combined with insignificant ideas is like harnessing a throughbred with an ass. You remember the farcical old school declamation, "A Midnight Murder," that proceeded in grandiose manner to a thrilling climax, and ended, "and relentlessly murdered, a mosquito!"

The pause, dramatically handled, always drew a laugh from the tolerant listeners. This is all very well in farce, but such anti-climax becomes painful when the speaker falls from the sublime to the ridiculous quite unintentionally. The pause, to be effective in some other manner than in that of the boomerang, must precede or follow a thought that is really worthwhile, or at least an idea whose bearing upon the rest of the speech is important.

□

7

Efficiency through Inflection

How soft the music of those village bells,
Falling at intervals upon the ear
In cadence sweet; now dying all away,
Now pealing loud again, and louder still,
Clear and sonorous, as the gale comes on!
With easy force it opens all the cells
Where Memory slept.

—**WILLIAM COWPER**, *The Task*

Herbert Spencer remarked that "Cadence", by which he meant the modulation of the tones of the voice in speaking, "is the running commentary of the emotions upon the propositions of the intellect." How true this is will appear when we reflect that the little upward and downward shadings of the voice tell more truly what we mean than our words. The expressiveness of language is literally multiplied by this subtle power to shade the vocal tones, and this voice-shading we call *inflection*.

The change of pitch *within* a word is even more important, because more delicate, than the change of pitch from phrase to phrase. Indeed, one cannot be practised without the other. The bare words are only so many bricks, inflection will make of them a pavement, a garage, or a cathedral. It is the power of inflection to change the meaning of words that gave birth to the old saying: "It is not so much what you say, as how you say it."

Mrs. Jameson, the Shakespearean commentator, has given us a penetrating example of the effect of inflection; "In her impersonation of the part of Lady Macbeth, Mrs. Siddons adopted successively three different intonations in giving the words 'We fail.' At first a quick contemptuous interrogation, 'We fail?' Afterwards, with the note of admiration, 'We fail,' an accent of indignant astonishment laying the principal emphasis on the word 'we', '*we fail*.' Lastly, she fixed on what I am convinced is the true reading, *We fail*, with the simple period, modulating the voice to a deep, low, resolute tone which settles the issue at once as though she had said: 'If we fail, why then we fail, and all is over.'"

This most expressive element of our speech is the last to be mastered in attaining to naturalness in speaking a foreign language, and its correct use is the main element in a natural, flexible utterance of our native tongue. Without varied inflections, speech becomes wooden and monotonous.

There are but two kinds of inflection, the rising and the falling, yet these two may be so shaded or so combined that they are capable of producing as many varieties of modulation as may be illustrated by either one or two lines, straight or curved, thus:

[Illustration of each line]
Sharp rising
Long rising
Level
Long falling
Sharp falling
Sharp rising and falling
Sharp falling and rising
Hesitating

These may be varied indefinitely, and serve merely to

illustrate what wide varieties of combination may be effected by these two simple inflections of the voice.

It is impossible to tabulate the various inflections which serve to express various shades of thought and feeling. A few suggestions are offered here, together with abundant exercises for practice, but the only real way to master inflection is to observe, experiment, and practice.

For example, take the common sentence, "Oh, he's all right." Note how a rising inflection may be made to express faint praise, or polite doubt, or uncertainty of opinion. Then note how the same words, spoken with a generally falling inflection may denote certainty, or good-natured approval, or enthusiastic praise, and so on.

In general, then, we find that a bending upward of the voice will suggest doubt and uncertainty, while a decided falling inflection will suggest that you are certain of your ground.

Students dislike to be told that their speeches are "not so bad," spoken with a rising inflection. To enunciate these words with a long falling inflection would endorse the speech rather heartily.

Say good-bye to an imaginary person whom you expect to see again tomorrow; then to a dear friend you never expect to meet again. Note the difference in inflection.

"I have had a delightful time," when spoken at the termination of a formal tea by a frivolous woman takes altogether different inflection than the same words spoken between lovers who have enjoyed themselves. Mimic the two characters in repeating this and observe the difference.

It must be made perfectly clear that inflection deals mostly in subtle, delicate shading *within single words*, and is not by any means accomplished by a general rise or fall in the voice in speaking a sentence. Yet certain sentences may be effectively delivered with just such inflection. Try this sentence in several ways, making no modulation until you come to the last two syllables, as indicated,

And yet I told him dis- (high) | tinctly. (low)

tinctly.
And yet I told him dis- | (high)
(low)

Now try this sentence by inflecting the important words so as to bring out various shades of meaning. The first forms, illustrated above, show change of pitch *within a single word*; the forms you will work out for yourself should show a number of such inflections throughout the sentence.

One of the chief means of securing emphasis is to employ a long falling inflection on the emphatic words, that is, to let the voice fall to a lower pitch on an *interior* vowel sound in a word. Try it on the words "every," and "destroy."

Be careful not to over-inflect. Too much modulation produces an unpleasant effect of artificiality, like a mature matron trying to be kittenish. It is a short step between true expression and unintentional burlesque. Scrutinise your own tones. Take a single expression like "Oh, no!" or "Oh, I see," or "Indeed," and by patient self-examination see how many shades of meaning may be expressed by inflection. This sort of common-sense practice will do you more good than a book of rules. *But don't forget to listen to your own voice.*

□

8

Concentration in Delivery

Attention is the microscope of the mental eye. Its power may be high or low; its field of view narrow or broad. When high power is used attention is confined within very circumscribed limits, but its action is exceedingly intense and absorbing. It sees but few things, but these few are observed "through and through" ... Mental energy and activity, whether of perception or of thought, thus concentrated, act like the sun's rays concentrated by the burning glass. The object is illumined, heated, set on fire. Impressions are so deep that they can never be effaced. Attention of this sort is the prime condition of the most productive mental labour.

—**DANIEL PUTNAM**, *Psychology*

Try to rub the top of your head forward and backward at the same time that you are patting your chest. Unless your powers of coordination are well developed, you will find it confusing, if not impossible. The brain needs special training before it can do two or more things efficiently at the same instant. It may seem like splitting a hair between its north and northwest corner, but some psychologists argue that *no* brain can think two distinct thoughts, absolutely simultaneously, that what seems to be simultaneous is really very rapid rotation from the first thought to the second and back again, just as in the above-cited experiment the attention must shift from one hand to the other until one or the other movement becomes partly or wholly automatic.

Whatever is the psychological truth of this contention, it is undeniable that the mind measurably loses grip on one idea the moment the attention is projected decidedly ahead to a second or a third idea.

A fault in public speakers that is as pernicious as it is common is that they try to think of the succeeding sentence while still uttering the former, and in this way their concentration trails off; in consequence, they start their sentences strongly and end them weakly. In a well-prepared written speech, the emphatic word usually comes at one end of the sentence. But an emphatic word needs emphatic expression, and this is precisely what it does not get when concentration flags by leaping too soon to that which is next to be uttered. Concentrate all your mental energies on the present sentence. Remember that the mind of your audience follows yours very closely, and if you withdraw your attention from what you are saying to what you are going to say, your audience will also withdraw theirs. They may not do so consciously and deliberately, but they will surely cease to give importance to the things that you yourself slight. It is fatal to the actor or the speaker to cross his bridges too soon.

Of course, all this is not to say that in the natural pauses of your speech you are not to take swift forward surveys, they are as important as the forward look in driving a motor car; the caution is of quite another sort: *while speaking one sentence do not think of the sentence to follow.* Let it come from its proper source, within yourself. You cannot deliver a broadside without concentrated force, that is what produces the explosion. In preparation you store and concentrate thought and feeling; in the pauses during delivery you swiftly look ahead and gather yourself for effective attack; during the moments of actual speech, *SPEAK, DON'T ANTICIPATE.* Divide your attention and you divide your power.

This matter of the effect of the inner man upon the outer needs a further word here, particularly as touching concentration.

"What do you read, my Lord?" Hamlet replied, "Words. Words. Words." That is a an age-old trouble. The mechanical calling of words is not expression, by a long stretch. Did you ever notice how hollow a memorised speech usually sounds? You have listened to the ranting, mechanical cadence of inefficient actors, lawyers and preachers. Their trouble is a mental one, they are not thinking with concentration thoughts that cause words to issue with sincerity and conviction, but are merely enunciating word-sounds mechanically. Painful experience alike to audience and to speaker! A parrot is equally eloquent. Again let Shakespeare instruct us, this tune in the insincere prayer of the King, Hamlet's uncle. He laments thus pointedly:

"My words fly up, my thoughts remain below:
Words without thoughts never to heaven go."

The truth is, that as a speaker your words must be born again every time they are spoken, then they will not suffer in their utterance, even though perforce committed to memory and repeated, like Dr. Russell Conwell's lecture, "Acres of Diamonds," five thousand times. Such speeches lose nothing by repetition for the perfectly patent reason that they arise from concentrated thought and feeling and not a mere necessity for saying something, which usually means anything, and that, in turn, is tantamount to nothing. If the thought beneath your words is warm, fresh, spontaneous, a part of your *self*, your utterance will have breath and life. Words are only a result. Do not try to get the result without stimulating the cause.

Do you ask *how* to concentrate? Think of the word itself,

and of its philological brother, *concentric*. Think of how a lens gathers and concented the rays of light within a given circle. It centres them by a process of withdrawal. It may seem like a harsh saying, but the man who cannot concentrate is either weak of will, a nervous wreck, or has never learned what will-power is good for.

You must concentrate by resolutely withdrawing your attention from everything else. If you concentrate your thought on a pain which may be afflicting you, that pain will grow more intense. "Count your blessings" and they will multiply. Centre your thought on your strokes and your tennis play will gradually improve. To concentrate is simply to attend to one thing, and attend to nothing else. If you find that you cannot do that, there is something wrong, attend to that first. Remove the cause and the symptom will disappear. Read the chapter on "Will Power." Cultivate your will by willing and then doing, at all costs. Concentrate, and you will win.

□

9

Force

> However, 'tis expedient to be wary:
> Indifference, certes, don't produce distress;
> And rash enthusiasm in good society
> Were nothing but a moral inebriety.
>
> —**BYRON**, *Don Juan.*

You have attended plays that seemed fair, yet they did not move you, grip you. In theatrical parlance, they failed to "get over," which means that their message did not get over the foot-lights to the audience. There was no punch, no jab to them, they had no force.

Of course, all this spells disaster, in big letters, not only in a stage production but in any platform effort. Every such presentation exists solely for the audience, and if it fails to hit them, and the expression is a good one, it has no excuse for living; nor will it live long.

What is Force?

Some of our most obvious words open up secret meanings under scrutiny, and this is one of them.

To begin with, we must recognize the distinction between inner and outer force. The one is cause, the other effect. The one is spiritual, the other physical. In this important particular, animate force differs from inanimate force, the power of man, coming from within and expressing itself outwardly, is of another sort from the force of Shimose powder, which awaits some influence from without to explode it. However susceptible to outside stimuli, the true source of power in man lies within himself. This may seem like "mere psychology," but it has an intensely practical bearing on public speaking, as will appear.

Not only must we discern the difference between human force and mere physical force, but we must not confuse its real essence with some of the things that may, and may not, accompany it. For example, loudness is not force, though force at times may be attended by noise. Mere roaring never made a good speech, yet there are moments, moments, mind you, not minutes, when big voice power may be used with tremendous effect.

Nor is violent motion force, yet force may result in violent motion.

Force is both a cause and an effect. Inner force, which must precede outer force, is a combination of four elements, acting progressively. First of all, *force arises from conviction*. You must be convinced of the truth, or the importance, or the meaning, of what you are about to say before you can give it forceful delivery. It must lay strong hold upon your convictions before it can grip your audience. Conviction convinces.

The Saturday Evening Post in an article on "England's T.R.", Winston Spencer Churchill, attributed much of Churchill's and Roosevelt's public platform success to their forceful delivery. No matter what is in hand, these men make themselves believe for the time being that that one thing is the most important on earth.

That kind of speaking wins, and it is that virile, strenuous, aggressive attitude which both distinguishes and maintains the platform careers of our greatest leaders.

But let us look a little closer at the origins of inner force. How does conviction affect the man who feels it? We have answered the inquiry in the very question itself, he *feels* it: *Conviction produces emotional tension*. Study the pictures of Theodore Roosevelt and of Billy Sunday in action, *action* is the word. Note the tension of their jaw muscles, the taut lines of sinews in their entire bodies when reaching a climax of force. Moral and physical force are alike in being both preceded and accompanied by *intensity*, tension, tightness of the cords of power.

It is this tautness of the bow-string, this knotting of the muscles, this contraction before the spring, that makes an audience *feel*, almost see, the reserve power in a speaker. In some really wonderful way it is more what a speaker does *not* say and do that reveals the dynamo within. *Anything* may come from such stored-up force once it is let loose; and that keeps an audience alert, hanging on the lips of a speaker for his next word. After all, it is all a question of manhood, for a stuffed doll has neither convictions nor emotional tension. If you are upholstered with sawdust, keep off the platform, for your own speech will puncture you.

Growing out of this conviction-tension comes *resolve to make the audience share that conviction-tension*. Purpose is the backbone of force; without it speech is flabby, it may glitter, but it is the iridescence of the spineless jellyfish. You must hold fast to your resolve if you would hold fast to your audience.

Finally, all this conviction-tension-purpose is lifeless and useless unless it results in *propulsion*. Let not your force "die a-borning,", bring it to full life in its conviction, emotional tension, resolve, and propulsive power.

Can Force be Acquired?

Yes, if the acquirer has any such capacities as we have just outlined. How to acquire this vital factor is suggested in its very analysis: Live with your subject until you are convinced of its importance.

If your message does not of itself arouse you to tension,

PULL yourself together. When a man faces the necessity of leaping across a crevasse he does not wait for inspiration, he *wills* his muscles into tensity for the spring, it is not without purpose that our English language uses the same word to depict a mighty though delicate steel contrivance and a quick leap through the air. Then resolve, and let it all end in actual *punch*.

This truth is worth reiteration: The man within is the final factor. He must supply the fuel. The audience, or even the man himself, may add the match, it matters little which, only so that there be fire. However skilfully your engine is constructed, however well it works, you will have no force if the fire has gone out under the boiler. It matters little how well you have mastered poise, pause, modulation, and tempo, if your speech lacks fire it is dead. Neither a dead engine nor a dead speech will move anybody.

Four factors of force are measurably within your control, and in that far may be acquired: *ideas, feeling about the subject, wording,* and *delivery*. Each of these is more or less fully discussed in this volume, except wording, which really requires a fuller rhetorical study than can here be ventured. It is, however, of the utmost importance that you should be aware of precisely how wording bears upon force in a sentence. Here are a few suggestions on the use of words to attain force:

Choice of Words

PLAIN words are more forceful than words less commonly used, *juggle* has more vigour than *prestidigitate*.

SHORT words are stronger than long words, *end* has more directness than *terminate*.

SAXON words are usually more forceful than Latinistic words, for force, use *wars against* rather than *militate against*.

SPECIFIC words are stronger than general words, *pressman* is more definite than *printer*.

CONNOTATIVE words, those that suggest more than they say, have more power than ordinary words, "She *let* herself be married" expresses more than "She *married*."

EPITHETS, figuratively descriptive words, are more effective than direct names, "Go tell that *old fox*," has more "punch" than "Go tell that *sly fellow*." ONOMATOPOETIC words, words that convey the sense by the sound, are more powerful than other words, *crash* is more effective than *cataclysm*.

Arrangement of words

Cut out modifiers.

Cut out connectives.

Begin with words that demand attention.

"End with words that deserve distinction," says Prof. Barrett Wendell.

Set strong ideas over against weaker ones, so as to gain strength by the contrast.

Avoid elaborate sentence structure, short sentences are stronger than long ones.

Cut out every useless word, so as to give prominence to the really important ones.

Let each sentence be a condensed battering ram, swinging to its final blow on the attention.

A familiar, homely idiom, if not worn by much use, is more effective than a highly formal, scholarly expression.

Consider well the relative value of different positions in the sentence so that you may give the prominent place to ideas you wish to emphasize.

"But," says someone, "is it not more honest to depend the inherent interest in a subject, its native truth, clearness and sincerity of presentation, and beauty of utterance, to win your audience? Why not charm men instead of capturing them by assault?"

Why Use Force?

There is much truth in such an appeal, but not all the truth. Clearness, persuasion, beauty, simple statement of truth, are all essential, indeed, they are all definite parts of a forceful presentment of a subject, without being the only parts. Strong meat may not be as attractive as ices, but all depends on the appetite and the stage of the meal.

You can not deliver an aggressive message with caressing little strokes. No! Jab it in with hard, swift solar plexus punches. You cannot strike fire from flint or from an audience with love taps. Say to a crowded theatre in a lackadaisical manner: "It seems to me that the house is on fire," and your announcement may be greeted with a laugh. If you flash out the words: "The house's on fire!" they will crush one another in getting to the exits.

The spirit and the language of force are definite with conviction. No immortal speech in literature contains such expressions as "it seems to me," "I should judge," "in my opinion," "I suppose," "perhaps it is true." The speeches that will live have been delivered by men ablaze with the courage of their convictions, who uttered their words as eternal truth. Of Jesus it was said that "the common people heard Him gladly." Why? "He taught them as one having *AUTHORITY*." An audience will never be moved by what "seems" to you to be truth or what in your "humble opinion" may be so. If you honestly can, assert convictions as your conclusions. Be sure you are right before you speak your speech, then utter your thoughts as though they were a Gibraltar of unimpeachable *truth*. Deliver them with the iron hand and confidence of a Cromwell. Assert them with the fire of authority. Pronounce them as an *ultimatum*. If you cannot speak with *conviction,* be silent.

What force did that young minister have who, fearing to be too dogmatic, thus exhorted his hearers: "My friends, as I assume that you are, it appears to be my duty to tell you that if you do not repent, so to speak, forsake your sins, as it were, and turn to righteousness, if I may so express it, you will be lost, in a measure"?

Effective speech must reflect the era. This is not a rose water age, and a tepid, half-hearted speech will not win. This is the century of trip hammers, of overland expresses that dash under cities and through mountain tunnels, and you must instil this spirit into your speech if you would move a popular audience. From a front seat listen to a first-class company present a modern drama, not a comedy, but a gripping, thrilling drama. Do not become absorbed in the story; reserve all your attention for the technique and the force of the acting. There is a kick and a crash as well as an infinitely subtle intensity in the big, climax-speeches that suggest this lesson: the same well-calculated, restrained, delicately shaded force would simply *rivet* your ideas in the minds of your audience. An air-gun will rattle bird-shot against a window pane, it takes a rifle to wing a bullet through plate glass and the oaken walls beyond.

When to Use Force

An audience is unlike the kingdom of heaven, the violent do not always take it by force. There are times when beauty and serenity should be the only bells in your chime. Force is only one of the great extremes of contrast, use neither it nor quiet utterance to the exclusion of other tones: be various, and in variety find even greater force than you could attain by attempting its constant use. If you are reading an essay on the beauties of the dawn, talking about the dainty bloom of a honey-suckle, or explaining the mechanism of a gas engine, a vigorous style of delivery is entirely out of place. But when you are appealing to wills and consciences for immediate action, forceful delivery wins. In such cases, consider the minds of your audience as so many safes that have been locked and the keys lost. Do not try to figure out the combinations. Pour a little nitro glycerine into the cracks and light the fuse. As these lines are being written a contractor down the street is clearing away the rocks with dynamite to lay the foundations for a great building. When you want to get action, do not fear to use dynamite.

The final argument for the effectiveness of force in public speech is the fact that everything must be enlarged for the purposes of the platform, that is why so few speeches read well in the reports on the morning after: statements appear crude and exaggerated because they are unaccompanied by the forceful delivery of a glowing speaker before an audience heated to attentive enthusiasm. So in preparing your speech you must not err on the side of mild statement, your audience will inevitably tone down your words in the cold grey of afterthought. When Phidias, the ancient Greek sculptor was criticised for the rough, bold outlines of a figure he had submitted in competition, he smiled and asked that his statue and the one wrought by his rival should be set upon the column for which the sculpture was destined. When this was done all the exaggerations and crudities, toned by distances, melted into exquisite grace of line and form. Each speech must be a special study in suitability and proportion.

Omit the thunder of delivery, if you will, but like Wendell Phillips put "silent lightning" into your speech. Make your thoughts breathe and your words burn. Birrell said: "Emerson writes like an electrical cat emitting sparks and shocks in every sentence." Go thou and speak likewise. Get the "big stick" into your delivery, be forceful.

□

10

Feeling and Enthusiasm

Enthusiasm is that secret and harmonious spirit that hovers over the production of genius.
—**ISAAC DISRAELI**, *Literary Character*

If you are addressing a body of scientists on such a subject as the veins in a butterfly's wings, or on road structure, naturally your theme will not arouse much feeling in either you or your audience. These are purely mental subjects. But if you want men to vote for a measure that will abolish child labour, or if you would inspire them to take up arms for freedom, you must strike straight at their feelings. We lie on soft beds, sit near the radiator on a cold day, eat cherry pie, and devote our attention to one of the opposite sex, not because we have reasoned out that it is the right thing to do, but because it feels right. No one but a dyspeptic chooses his diet from a chart. Our feelings dictate what we shall eat and generally how we shall act. Man is a feeling animal, hence the public speaker's ability to arouse men to action depends almost wholly on his ability to touch their emotions.

Negro mothers on the auction-block seeing their children sold away from them into slavery have flamed out some of America's most stirring speeches. True, the mother did not have any knowledge of the technique of speaking, but she had something greater than all technique, more effective than reason feeling. The great speeches of the world have not been delivered on tariff reductions or post-office appropriations. The speeches that will live have been charged with emotional force. Prosperity and peace are poor developers of eloquence. When great wrongs are to be righted, when the public heart is flaming with passion, that is the occasion for memorable speaking. Patrick Henry made an immortal address, for in an epochal crisis he pleaded for liberty. He had roused himself to the point where he could honestly and passionately exclaim, "Give me liberty or give me death." His fame would have been different had he lived today and argued for the recall of judges.

The Power of Enthusiasm

Political parties hire bands, and pay for applause, they argue that, for vote-getting, to stir up enthusiasm is more effective than reasoning. How far they are right depends on the hearers, but there can be no doubt about the contagious nature of enthusiasm. A watch manufacturer tried out two series of watch advertisements; one argued the superior construction, workmanship, durability, and guarantee offered with the watch; the other was headed, "A Watch to be Proud of," and dwelt upon the pleasure and pride of ownership. The latter series sold twice as many as the former. A salesman for a locomotive works informed the writer that in selling railroad engines emotional appeal was stronger than an argument based on mechanical excellence.

Illustrations without number might be cited to show that in all our actions we are emotional beings. The speaker who would speak efficiently must develop the power to arouse feeling.

Webster, great debater that he was, knew that the real secret of a speaker's power was an emotional one. He eloquently says of eloquence:

"Affected passion, intense expression, the pomp of

declamation, all may aspire after it; they cannot reach it. It comes, if it comes at all, like the outbreak of a fountain from the earth, or the bursting forth of volcanic fires, with spontaneous, original, native force".

"The graces taught in the schools, the costly ornaments and studied contrivances of speech, shock and disgust men, when their own lives, and the fate of their wives, their children, and their country hang on the decision of the hour. Then words have lost their power, rhetoric is in vain, and all elaborate oratory contemptible. Even genius itself then feels rebuked and subdued, as in the presence of higher qualities. Then patriotism is eloquent, then self-devotion is eloquent. The clear conception outrunning the deductions of logic, the high purpose, the firm resolve, the dauntless spirit, speaking on the tongue, beaming from the eye, informing every feature, and urging the whole man onward, right onward to his subject, this, is eloquence; or rather, it is something greater and higher than all eloquence; it is action, noble, sublime, godlike action."

One of the present writers strolled up a village street after dinner and noticed a crowd listening to a "faker" speaking on a corner from a goods-box. Remembering Emerson's advice about learning something from every man we meet, the observer stopped to listen to this speaker's appeal. He was selling a hair tonic, which he claimed to have discovered in Arizona. He removed his hat to show what this remedy had done for him, washed his face in it to demonstrate that it was as harmless as water, and enlarged on its merits in such an enthusiastic manner that the half-dollars poured in on him in a silver flood. When he had supplied the audience with hair tonic, he asked why a greater proportion of men than women were bald. No one knew. He explained that it was because women wore thinner-soled shoes, and so made a good electrical connection with Mother Earth, while men wore thick, dry-soled shoes that did not transmit the earth's electricity to the body. Men's hair, not having a proper amount of electrical food, died and fell out. Of course he had a remedy, a little copper plate that should be nailed on the bottom of the shoe. He pictured in enthusiastic and vivid terms the desirability of escaping baldness, and paid tributes to his copper plates. Strange as it may seem when the story is told in cold print, the speaker's enthusiasm had swept his audience with him, and they crushed around his stand with outstretched "quarters" in their anxiety to be the possessors of these magical plates!

Emerson's suggestion had been well taken, the observer had seen again the wonderful, persuasive power of enthusiasm!

Listen! Emerson said: "Nothing great was ever achieved without enthusiasm." Carlyle declared that "Every great movement in the annals of history has been the triumph of enthusiasm." It is as contagious as measles. Eloquence is half inspiration. Sweep your audience with you in a pulsation of enthusiasm. Let yourself go. "A man," said Oliver Cromwell, "never rises so high as when he knows not whither he is going."

How are We to Acquire and Develop Enthusiasm?

It is not to be slipped on like a jacket. A book cannot furnish you with it. It is a growth, an effect. But an effect of what? Let us see.

Emerson wrote: "A painter told me that nobody could draw a tree without in some sort becoming a tree; or draw a child by studying the outlines of his form merely, but, by watching for a time his motion and plays, the painter enters his nature, and then can draw him at will in every attitude. I knew a draughtsman employed in a public survey, who found that he could not sketch the rocks until their geological structure was first explained to him."

When Sarah Bernhardt played a difficult role frequently she would speak to no one from four o'clock in the afternoon until after the performance. From the hour of four she lived her character. Booth, it is reported, would not permit anyone to speak to him between the acts of his Shakesperean roles, for he was Macbeth then, not Booth. Dante, exiled from his beloved Florence, condemned to death, lived in caves, half starved; then Dante wrote out his heart in "The Divine Comedy." Bunyan entered into the spirit of his "Pilgrim's Progress" so thoroughly that he fell down on the floor of Bedford jail and wept for joy. Turner, who lived in a garret, arose before daybreak and walked over the hills nine miles to see the sun rise on the ocean, that he might catch the spirit of its wonderful beauty. Wendell Phillips' sentences were full of "silent lightning" because he bore in his heart the sorrow of five million slaves.

There is only one way to get feeling into your speaking, and whatever else you forget, forget not this: *You must actually ENTER INTO* the character you impersonate, the cause you advocate, the case you argue, enter into it so deeply that it clothes you, enthralls you, possesses you wholly. Then you are, in the true meaning of the word, in *sympathy* with your subject, for its feeling is your feeling, you "feel with" it, and therefore your enthusiasm is both genuine and contagious. The Carpenter who spoke as "never man spake" uttered words born out of a passion of love for humanity, he had entered into humanity, and thus became Man.

But we must not look upon the foregoing words as a facile prescription for decocting a feeling which may then be ladled out to a complacent audience in quantities to suit the need of the moment. Genuine feeling in a speech is bone and blood of the speech itself and not something that may be added to it or subtracted at will. In the ideal address theme, speaker and audience become one, fused by the emotion and thought of the hour.

The Need of Sympathy for Humanity

It is impossible to lay too much stress on the necessity for the speaker's having a broad and deep tenderness for human nature. One of Victor Hugo's biographers attributes his power as an orator and writer to his wide sympathies and profound religious feelings. Recently we heard once the editor of *Collier's Weekly* spoke on short-story writing, and he so often emphasized the necessity for this broad love for humanity, this truly religious feeling, that he apologised twice for delivering a sermon. Few if any of the immortal speeches were ever delivered for a selfish or a narrow cause, they were born out of a passionate desire to help humanity. The seal and sign of greatness is a desire to serve others. Self-preservation is the first law of life, but self-abnegation is the first law of greatness, and of art. Selfishness is the fundamental cause of all sin, it is the thing that all great religions, all worthy philosophies, have struck at. Out of a heart of real sympathy and love come the speeches that move humanity.

As Webster said, it is of no use to try to pretend sympathy or feelings. It cannot be done successfully. "Nature is forever putting a premium on reality." What is false is soon detected as such. The thoughts and feelings that create and mould the speech in the study must be born again when the speech is delivered from the platform. Do not let your words say one thing, and your voice and attitude another. There is no room here for half-hearted, nonchalant methods of delivery. Sincerity is the very soul of eloquence. Carlyle was right: "No Mirabeau, Napoleon, Burns, Cromwell, no man adequate to do anything, but is first of all in right earnest about it; what I call a sincere man. I should say sincerity, a great, deep, genuine sincerity, is the first characteristic of all men in any way heroic. Not the sincerity that calls itself sincere; ah no, that is a very poor matter indeed; a shallow braggart, conscious sincerity, oftenest self-conceit mainly. The great man's sincerity is of the kind he cannot speak of, is not conscious of."

□

11

Fluency through Preparation

> In omnibus negotiis prius quam aggrediare, adhibenda est praeparatio diligens, In all matters before beginning a diligent preparation should be made.
>
> —CICERO, *De Officiis*

Take your dictionary and look up the words that contain the Latin stem *flu* – the results will be suggestive.

At first blush it would seem that fluency consists in a ready, easy use of words. Not so, the flowing quality of speech is much more, for it is a composite effect, with each of its prior conditions deserving of careful notice.

The Sources of Fluency

Speaking broadly, fluency is almost entirely a matter of preparation. Certainly, native gifts figure largely here, as in every art, but even natural facility is dependent on the very same laws of preparation that hold good for the man of supposedly small native endowment. Let this encourage you if, like Moses, you are prone to complain that you are not a ready speaker.

Have you ever stopped to analyse that expression, "a ready speaker?" Readiness, in its prime sense, is preparedness, and they are most ready who are best prepared. Quick firing depends more on the alert finger than on the hair trigger. Your fluency will be in direct ratio to two important conditions: your knowledge of what you are going to say, and your being accustomed to telling what you know to an audience. This gives us the second great element of fluency, to preparation must be added the ease that arises from practice; of which more presently.

Knowledge is Essential

But preparation goes beyond the getting of the facts in the case you are to present: it includes also the ability to think and arrange your thoughts, a full and precise vocabulary, an easy manner of speech and breathing, absence of self-consciousness, and the several other characteristics of efficient delivery that have deserved special attention in other parts of this book rather than in this chapter.

Preparation may be either general or specific; usually it should be both. A life-time of reading, of companionship with stirring thoughts, of wrestling with the problems of life, this constitutes a general preparation of inestimable worth. Out of a well-stored mind, and, richer still, a broad experience, and, best of all, a warmly sympathetic heart, the speaker will have to draw much material that no *immediate* study could provide. General preparation consists of all that a man has put into himself, all that heredity and environment have instilled into him, and, that other rich source of preparedness for speech, the friendship of wise companions. Proper friendships form one of the best means for the formation of ideas and ideals, for they enable one to practise in giving expression to thought. The speaker who would speak fluently before an audience should learn to speak fluently and entertainingly with a friend. Clarify your ideas by putting them in words; the talker gains as much from his conversation as the listener. You sometimes begin to converse on a subject thinking you have very little to say, but one idea gives birth to another, and you are surprised to learn that the more you give the more you have to give. This give-and-take of friendly conversation develops mentality, and fluency in expression. Longfellow said: "A single conversation across the table with a wise man is better than ten years' study of books," and Holmes whimsically yet none the less truthfully declared that half the time he talked to find out what he thought. But that method must not be applied on the platform!

After all this enrichment of life by storage, must come the special preparation for the particular speech. This is of so definite a sort that it warrants separate chapter-treatment later.

Practice

But preparation must also be of another sort than the gathering, organising, and shaping of materials, it must include *practice*, which, like mental preparation, must be both general and special.

Do not feel surprised or discouraged if practice on the principles of delivery herein laid down seems to retard your fluency. For a time, this will be inevitable. While you are working for proper inflection, for instance, inflection will be demanding your first thoughts, and the flow of your speech, for the time being, will be secondary. This warning, however, is strictly for the closet, for your practice at home. Do not carry any thoughts of inflection with you to the platform. There you must *think* only of your subject. There is an absolute telepathy between the audience and the speaker. If your thought goes to your gesture, their thought will too. If your interest goes to the quality of your voice, they will be regarding that instead of what your voice is uttering.

You have doubtless been adjured to "forget everything but your subject." This advice says either too much or too little. The truth is that while on the platform you must not *forget* a great many things that are not in your subject, but you must not *think* of them. Your attention must consciously go only to your message, but subconsciously you will be attending to the points of technique which have become more or less *habitual by practice*.

A nice balance between these two kinds of attention is important.

You can no more escape this law than you can live without air: Your platform gestures, your voice, your inflection, will all be just as good as your *habit* of gesture, voice, and inflection makes them, no better. Even the thought of whether you are speaking fluently or not will have the effect of marring your flow of speech.

Return to the opening chapter, on self-confidence, and again lay its precepts to heart. Learn by rules to speak without thinking of rules. It is not, or ought not to be, necessary for you to stop to think how to say the alphabet correctly, as a matter of fact it is slightly more difficult for you to repeat Z, Y, X than it is to say X, Y, Z, habit has established the order. Just so you must master the laws of efficiency in speaking until it is a second nature for you to speak correctly rather than otherwise. A beginner at the piano has a great deal of trouble with the mechanics of playing, but as time goes on his fingers become trained and almost instinctively wander over the keys correctly. As an inexperienced speaker you will find a great deal of difficulty at first in putting principles into practice, for you will be scared, like the young swimmer, and make some crude strokes, but if you persevere you will "win out."

Thus, to sum up, the vocabulary you have enlarged by study, the ease in speaking you have developed by practice, the economy of your well-studied emphasis will all subconsciously come to your aid on the platform. Then the habits you have formed will be earning you a splendid dividend. The fluency of your speech will be at the speed of flow your practice has made habitual.

But this means work. What good habit does not? No

philosopher's stone that will act as a substitute for laborious practice has ever been found. If it were, it would be thrown away, because it would kill our greatest joy, the delight of acquisition. If public-speaking means to you a fuller life, you will know no greater happiness than a well-spoken speech. The time you have spent in gathering ideas and in private practice of speaking you will find amply rewarded.

□

12

The Voice

> Oh, there is something in that voice that reaches The innermost recesses of my spirit!
>
> —**LONGFELLOW**, *Christus*

The dramatic critic of *The London Times* once declared that acting is nine-tenths voice work. Leaving the message aside, the same may justly be said of public speaking. A rich, correctly-used voice is the greatest physical factor of persuasiveness and power, often over-topping the effects of reason.

But a good voice, well handled, is not only an effective possession for the professional speaker, it is a mark of personal culture as well, and even a distinct commercial asset. Gladstone, himself the possessor of a deep, musical voice, has said: "Ninety men in every hundred in the crowded professions will probably never rise above mediocrity because the training of the voice is entirely neglected and considered of no importance." These are words worth-pondering.

There are three fundamental requisites for a good voice:

1. Ease

The secret of good voice is relaxation; and this is true, for relaxation is the basis of ease. The air waves that produce voice result in a different kind of tone when striking against relaxed muscles than when striking constricted muscles. Try this for yourself. Contract the muscles of your face and throat as you do in hate, and flame out "I hate you!" Now relax as you do when thinking gentle, tender thoughts, and say, "I love you." How different the voice sounds.

In practising voice exercises, and in speaking, never force your tones. Ease must be your watchword. The voice is a delicate instrument, and you must not handle it with hammer and tongs. Don't *make* your voice go, *let* it go. Don't work. Let the yoke of speech be easy and its burden light.

Your throat should be free from strain during speech, therefore it is necessary to avoid muscular contraction. The throat must act as a sort of chimney or funnel for the voice, hence any unnatural constriction will not only harm its tones but injure its health.

Nervousness and mental strain are common sources of mouth and throat constriction, so make the battle for poise and self-confidence for which we pleaded in the opening chapter.

But *how* can I relax? you ask. By simply *willing* to relax. Hold your arm out straight from your shoulder. Now, withdraw all power and let it fall. Practise relaxation of the muscles of the throat by letting your neck and head fall forward. Roll the upper part of your body around, with the waist line acting as a pivot. Let your head fall and roll around as you shift the torso to different positions. Do not force your head around, simply relax your neck and let gravity pull it around as your body moves.

Again, let your head fall forward on your breast; raise your head, letting your jaw hang. Relax until your jaw feels heavy, as though it were a weight hung to your face. Remember, you must relax the jaw to obtain command of it. It must be free and flexible for the moulding of tone, and to let the tone pass out unobstructed.

The lips also must be made flexible, to aid in the moulding of clear and beautiful tones. For flexibility of lips repeat the syllables, *mo, me*. In saying *mo,* bring the lips up to resemble the shape of the letter O. In repeating *me* draw them back as you do in a grin. Repeat this exercise rapidly, giving the lips as much exercise as possible.

Try the following exercise in the same manner:

Mo, E, O, E, OO, Ah.

After this exercise has been mastered, the following will also be found excellent for flexibility of lips:

Memorise these *sounds* indicated (not the *expressions*) so that you can repeat them rapidly.

A as in May.	E as in Met.	U as in Use.
A " Ah.	I " Ice.	Oi " Oil.
A " At.	I " It.	Ou " Our.
O " No.	O " No.	OO " Ooze.
A " All.	OO " Foot.	A " Ah.
E " Eat.	OO " Ooze.	E " Eat.

All the activity of breathing must be centred, not in the throat, but in the middle of the body, you must breathe from the diaphragm. Note the way you breathe when lying flat on the back, undressed in bed. You will observe that all the activity then centred around the diaphragm. This is the natural and correct method of breathing. By constant watchfulness make this your habitual manner, for it will enable you to relax more perfectly the muscles of the throat.

The next fundamental requisite for good voice is:

2. Openness

If the muscles of the throat are constricted, the tone passage partially closed, and the mouth kept half-shut, how can you expect the tone to come out bright and clear, or even to come out at all? Sound is a series of waves, and if you make a prison of your mouth, holding the jaws and lips rigidly, it will be very difficult for the tone to squeeze through, and even when it does escape it will lack force and carrying power. Open your mouth wide, relax all the organs of speech, and let the tone flow out easily.

Start to yawn, but instead of yawning, speak while your throat is open. Make this open-feeling habitual when speaking, we say *make* because it is a matter of resolution and of practice, if your vocal organs are healthy. Your tone passages may be partly closed by enlarged tonsils, adenoids, or enlarged turbinate bones of the nose. If so, a skilled physician should be consulted.

The nose is an important tone passage and should be kept open and free for perfect tones. What we call "talking through the nose" is not talking through the nose, as you can easily demonstrate by holding your nose as you talk. If you are bothered with nasal tones caused by growths or swellings in the nasal passages, a slight, painless operation will remove the obstruction. This is quite important, aside from voice, for the general health will be much lowered if the lungs are continually starved for air.

The final fundamental requisite for good voice is:

3. Forwardness

A voice that is pitched back in the throat is dark, sombre, and unattractive. The tone must be pitched forward, but do not *force* it forward. You will recall that our first principle was ease. *Think* the tone forward and out. Believe it is going forward, and allow it to flow easily. You can tell whether you are placing your tone forward or not by inhaling a deep breath and singing *ah* with the mouth wide open, trying to feel the little delicate sound waves strike the bony arch of the mouth just above the front teeth. The sensation is so slight that you will probably not be able to detect it at once, but persevere in your practice, always thinking the tone forward, and you will be rewarded by feeling your voice strike the roof of your mouth. A correct forward-placing of the tone will do away with the dark, throaty tones that are so unpleasant, inefficient, and harmful to the throat.

Close the lips, humming *ng, im, or, an.* Think the tone forward. Do you feel it strike the lips?

Hold the palm of your hand in front of your face and say vigorously *crash, dash, whirl, buzz.* Can you feel the forward tones strike against your hand? Practice until you can. Remember, the only way to get your voice forward is to *put* it forward.

How to Develop the Carrying Power of the Voice

It is not necessary to speak loudly in order to be heard at a distance. It is necessary only to speak correctly. A paper rustling on the stage of a large auditorium can be heard distinctly in the furthermost seat in the gallery. If you will only use your voice correctly, you will not have much difficulty in being heard. Of course it is always well to address your speech to your furthest listeners; if they get it, those nearer will have no trouble, but aside from this obvious suggestion, you must observe these laws of voice production:

Remember to apply the principles of ease, openness and forwardness, they are the prime factors in enabling your voice to be heard at a distance.

Do not gaze at the floor as you talk. This habit not only gives the speaker an amateurish appearance but if the head is hung forward the voice will be directed towards the ground instead of floating out over the audience.

Voice is a series of air vibrations. To strengthen it two things are necessary: more air or breath, and more vibration.

Breath is the very basis of voice. As a bullet with little powder behind it will not have force and carrying power, so the voice that has little breath behind it will be weak. Not only will deep breathing, breathing from the diaphragm, give the voice a better support, but it will give it a stronger resonance by improving the general health.

Usually, ill health means a weak voice, while abundant physical vitality is shown through a strong, vibrant voice.

Therefore anything that improves the general vitality is an excellent voice strengthener, provided you *use* the voice properly. Authorities differ on most of the rules of hygiene but on one point they all agree: vitality and longevity are increased by deep breathing. Practice this until it becomes second nature. Whenever you are speaking, take in deep breaths, but in such a manner that the inhalations will be silent.

Do not try to speak too long without renewing your breath. Nature cares for this pretty well unconsciously in conversation, and she will do the same for you in platform speaking if you do not interfere with her premonitions.

A certain very successful speaker developed voice carrying power by running across country, practicing his speeches as he went. The vigorous exercise forced him to take deep breaths, and developed lung power. A hard-fought basketball or tennis game is an efficient way of practicing deep breathing. When these methods are not convenient, we recommend the following:

Place your hands at your sides, on the waist line.

By trying to encompass your waist with your fingers and thumbs, force all the air out of the lungs.

Take a deep breath. Remember, all the activity is to be centred in the *middle* of the body; do not raise the shoulders. As the breath is taken, your hands will be forced out.

Repeat the exercise, placing your hands on the small of the back and forcing them out as you inhale.

Many methods for deep breathing have been given by various authorities. Get the air into your lungs, that is the important thing.

The body acts as a sounding board for the voice just as the body of the violin acts as a sounding board for its tones. You can increase its vibrations by practice.

Place your finger on your lip and hum the musical scale, thinking and placing the voice forward on the lips. Do you feel the lips vibrate? After a little practice they will vibrate, giving a tickling sensation.

Repeat this exercise, throwing the humming sound into the nose. Hold the upper part of the nose between the thumb and forefinger. Can you feel the nose vibrate?

Placing the palm of your hand on top of your head, repeat this humming exercise. Think the voice there as you hum in head tones. Can you feel the vibration there?

Now place the palm of your hand on the back of your head, repeating the foregoing process. Then try it on the chest. Always remember to think your tone where you desire to feel the vibrations. The mere act of thinking about any portion of your body will tend to make it vibrate.

Repeat the following, after a deep inhalation, endeavouring to feel all portions of your body vibrate at the same time. When you have attained this, you will find that it is a pleasant sensation.

What ho, my jovial mates. Come on! We will frolic it like fairies, frisking in the merry moonshine.

Purity of Voice

This quality is sometimes destroyed by wasting the breath. Carefully control the breath, using only as much as is necessary for the production of tone. Utilize all that you give out. Failure to do this results in a breathy tone. Take in breath like a prodigal; in speaking, give it out like a miser.

Voice Suggestions

Never attempt to force your voice when hoarse.

Do not drink cold water when speaking. The sudden shock to the heated organs of speech will injure the voice.

Avoid pitching your voice too high, it will make it raspy. This is a common fault. When you find your voice in too high a range, lower it. Do not wait until you get to the platform to try this. Practice it in your daily conversation. Repeat the alphabet, beginning A on the lowest scale possible and going up a note on each succeeding letter, for the development of range. A wide range will give you facility in making numerous changes of pitch.

Do not form the habit of listening to your voice when speaking. You will need your brain to think of what you are saying, reserve your observation for private practice.

□

13

Voice Charm

> A cheerful temper joined with innocence will make beauty attractive, knowledge delightful, and wit good-natured.
>
> —**JOSEPH ADDISON**, *The Tattler*

Poe said that "the tone of beauty is sadness," but he was evidently thinking from cause to effect, not contrariwise, for sadness is rarely a producer of beauty, that is peculiarly the province of joy.

The exquisite beauty of a sunset is not exhilarating but tends to a sort of melancholy that is not far from delight. The haunting beauty of deep, quiet music holds more than a tinge of sadness. The lovely minor cadences of bird song at twilight are almost depressing.

The reason we are affected to sadness by certain forms of placid beauty is two-fold: movement is stimulating and joy-producing, while quietude leads to reflection, and reflection in turn often brings out the tone of regretful longing for that which is past; secondly, quiet beauty produces a vague aspiration for the relatively unattainable, yet does not stimulate to the tremendous effort necessary to make the dimly desired state or object ours.

We must distinguish, for these reasons, between the

sadness of beauty and the joy of beauty. True, joy is a deep, inner thing and takes in much more than the idea of bounding, sanguine spirits, for it includes a certain active contentedness of heart. In this chapter, however the word will have its optimistic, exuberant connotation, we are thinking now of vivid, bright-eyed, laughing joy.

Musical, joyous tones constitute voice charm, a subtle magnetism that is delightfully contagious. Now it might seem to the desultory reader that to take the lancet and cut into this alluring voice quality would be to dissect a butterfly wing and so destroy its charm. Yet how can we induce an effect if we are not certain as to the cause?

Nasal Resonance Produces the Bell-tones of the Voice

The tone passages of the nose must be kept entirely free for the bright tones of voice, and after our warning in the preceding chapter you will not confuse what is popularly and erroneously called a "nasal" tone with the true nasal quality, which is so well illustrated by the voice work of trained French singers and speakers.

To develop nasal resonance sing the following, dwelling as long as possible on the *ng* sounds. Pitch the voice in the nasal cavity. Practice both in high and low registers, and develop range, *with brightness*.

'Sing-song. Ding-dong. Hong-kong. Long-thong'.

Practice in the falsetto voice develops a bright quality in the normal speaking-voice. Try the following, and any other selections you choose, in a falsetto voice. A man's falsetto voice is extremely high and womanish, so men should not practice in falsetto after the exercise becomes tiresome.

'She perfectly scorned the best of his clan, and declared' the ninth of any man, a perfectly vulgar fraction.'

The actress Mary Anderson asked the poet Longfellow what she could do to improve her voice. He replied, "Read aloud daily, joyous, lyric poetry."

The joyous tones are the bright tones. Develop them by exercise. Practice your voice exercises in an attitude of joy. Under the influence of pleasure the body expands, the tone passages open, the action of heart and lungs is accelerated, and all the primary conditions for good tone are established.

Happiness is largely an attitude of mind, of viewing life from the right angle. The optimistic attitude can be cultivated, and it will express itself in voice charm. A telephone company recently placarded this motto in their booths: "The Voice with the Smile Wins." It does. Try it.

Reading joyous prose, or lyric poetry, will help put smile and joy of soul into your voice. The following selections are excellent for practice.

REMEMBER that when you first practice these classics you are to give sole attention to two things: a joyous attitude of heart and body, and bright tones of voice. After these ends have been attained to your satisfaction, carefully review the principles of public speaking laid down in the preceding chapters and put them into practice as you read these passages again and again. *It would be better to commit each selection to memory.*

Selection For Practice From Miltons's *"L' Allegro"*

Haste thee, Nymph, and bring with thee
Jest, and youthful Jollity,
Quips and Cranks and wanton Wiles,
Nods and Becks, and wreathed Smiles,
Such as hang on Hebe's cheek,
And love to live in dimple sleek,
Sport that wrinkled Care derides,
And Laughter holding both his sides.
Come, and trip it as ye go
On the light fantastic toe;
And in thy right hand lead with thee
The mountain nymph, sweet Liberty:

And, if I give thee honour due,
Mirth, admit me of thy crew,
To live with her, and live with thee,
In unreproved pleasures free;
To hear the lark begin his flight,
And singing, startle the dull Night
From his watch-tower in the skies,
Till the dappled Dawn doth rise;
Then to come in spite of sorrow,
And at my window bid good-morrow
Through the sweetbrier, or the vine,
Or the twisted eglantine;
While the cock with lively din
Scatters the rear of darkness thin,
And to the stack, or the barn-door,
Stoutly struts his dames before;
Oft listening how the hounds and horn
Cheerly rouse the slumbering Morn,
From the side of some hoar hill,
Through the high wood echoing shrill;
Sometime walking, not unseen,
By hedge-row elms, on hillocks green,
Right against the eastern gate,
Where the great Sun begins his state,
Robed in flames and amber light,
The clouds in thousand liveries dight,
While the ploughman near at hand
Whistles o'er the furrowed land,
And the milkmaid singing blithe,
And the mower whets his scythe,
And every shepherd tells his tale,
Under the hawthorn in the dale.

The Sea

The sea, the sea, the open sea,
The blue, the fresh, the fever free;
Without a mark, without a bound,
It runneth the earth's wide regions round;
It plays with the clouds, it mocks the skies,
Or like a cradled creature lies.
I'm on the sea, I'm on the sea,
I am where I would ever be,
With the blue above and the blue below,
And silence wheresoe'er I go.
If a storm should come and awake the deep,
What matter? I shall ride and sleep.
I love, oh! how I love to ride
On the fierce, foaming, bursting tide,
Where every mad wave drowns the moon,
And whistles aloft its tempest tune,
And tells how goeth the world below,
And why the southwest wind doth blow!
I never was on the dull, tame shore
But I loved the great sea more and more,
And backward flew to her billowy breast,
Like a bird that seeketh her mother's nest,
And a mother she was and is to me,
For I was born on the open sea.
The waves were white, and red the morn,
In the noisy hour when I was born;
The whale it whistled, the porpoise rolled,
And the dolphins bared their backs of gold;
And never was heard such an outcry wild,
As welcomed to life the ocean child.
I have lived, since then, in calm and strife,
Full fifty summers a rover's life,
With wealth to spend, and a power to range,
But never have sought or sighed for change:

And death, whenever he comes to me,
Shall come on the wide, unbounded sea!

—**BARRY CORNWALL**

The sun does not shine for a few trees and flowers, but for the wide world's joy. The lonely pine upon the mountain-top waves its sombre boughs, and cries, "Thou art my sun." And the little meadow violet lifts its cup of blue, and whispers with its perfumed breath, "Thou art my sun." And the grain in a thousand fields rustles in the wind, and makes answer, "Thou art my sun." And so God sits effulgent in Heaven, not for a favoured few, but for the universe of life; and there is no creature so poor or so low that he may not look up with child-like confidence and say, "My Father! Thou art mine."

—**HENRY WARD BEECHER**

The Lark

Bird of the wilderness,
Blithesome and cumberless,
Sweet be thy matin o'er moorland and lea!
Emblem of happiness,
Blest is thy dwelling-place:
Oh, to abide in the desert with thee!
Wild is thy lay, and loud,
Far in the downy cloud,
Love gives it energy; love gave it birth.
Where, on thy dewy wing,
Where art thou journeying?
Thy lay is in heaven; thy love is on earth.
O'er fell and fountain sheen,
O'er moor and mountain green,
O'er the red streamer that heralds the day;
Over the cloudlet dim,
Over the rainbow's rim,
Musical cherub, soar, singing, away!

Then, when the gloaming comes,
Low in the heather blooms,
Sweet will thy welcome and bed of love be!
Emblem of happiness,
Blest is thy dwelling-place.
Oh, to abide in the desert with thee!

—**JAMES HOGG**

In joyous conversation there is an elastic touch, a delicate stroke, upon the central ideas, generally following a pause. This elastic touch adds vivacity to the voice. If you try repeatedly, it can be sensed by feeling the tongue strike the teeth. The entire absence of elastic touch in the voice can be observed in the thick tongue of the intoxicated man. Try to talk with the tongue lying still in the bottom of the mouth, and you will obtain largely the same effect. Vivacity of utterance is gained by using the tongue to strike off the emphatic idea with a decisive, elastic touch.

Deliver the following with decisive strokes on the emphatic ideas. Deliver it in a vivacious manner, noting the elastic touch-action of the tongue. A flexible, responsive tongue is absolutely essential to good voice work.

The Brook

I come from haunts of coot and hern,
I make a sudden sally,
And sparkle out among the fern,
To bicker down a valley.
By thirty hills I hurry down,
Or slip between the ridges;
By twenty thorps, a little town,
And half a hundred bridges.
Till last by Philip's farm I flow
To join the brimming river;
For men may come and men may go,

But I go on forever.
I chatter over stony ways,
In little sharps and trebles,
I bubble into eddying bays,
I babble on the pebbles.
With many a curve my banks I fret,
By many a field and fallow,
And many a fairy foreland set,
With willow-weed and mallow.
I chatter, chatter, as I flow,
To join the brimming river;
For men may come and men may go,
But I go on forever.
I wind about, and in and out,
With here a blossom sailing,
And here and there a lusty trout,
And here and there a grayling,
And here and there a foamy flake,
Upon me, as I travel,
With many a silvery water-break,
Above the golden gravel,
And draw them all along, and flow,
To join the brimming river,
For men may come and men may go,
But I go on forever.
I steal by lawns and grassy plots,
I slide by hazel covers,
I move the sweet forget-me-nots
That grow for happy lovers.
I slip, I slide, I gloom, I glance,
Among my skimming swallows;
I make the netted sunbeam dance,
Against my sandy shallows,
I murmur under moon and stars,
In brambly wildernesses,

I linger by my shingly bars,
I loiter round my cresses;
And out again I curve and flow,
To join the brimming river;
For men may come and men may go,
But I go on forever.

—**ALFRED TENNYSON**

The children at play on the street, glad from sheer physical vitality, display a resonance and charm in their voices quite different from the voices that float through the silent halls of the hospitals. A skilled physician can tell much about his patient's condition from the mere sound of the voice. Failing health, or even physical weariness, tells through the voice. It is always well to rest and be entirely refreshed before attempting to deliver a public address. As to health, neither scope nor space permits us to discuss here the laws of hygiene. There are many excellent books on this subject. In the reign of the Roman emperor Tiberius, one senator wrote to another: "To the wise, a word is sufficient."

"The apparel oft proclaims the man;" the voice always does, it is one of the greatest revealers of character. The superficial woman, the brutish man, the reprobate, the person of culture, often discloses inner nature in the voice, for even the cleverest dissembler cannot entirely prevent its tones and qualities being affected by the slightest change of thought or emotion. In anger it becomes high, harsh, and unpleasant; in love low, soft, and melodious, the variations are as limitless as they are fascinating to observe. Visit a theatrical hotel in a large city, and listen to the buzz-saw voices of the chorus girls from some burlesque "attraction." The explanation is simple, buzz-saw lives. Emerson said: "When a man lives with God his voice shall be as sweet as the murmur of the brook or the rustle of the corn." It is impossible to think selfish thoughts and have either an attractive personality, a lovely character, or a charming voice. If you want to possess voice charm, cultivate a deep, sincere sympathy for mankind. Love will shine out through your eyes and proclaim itself in your tones. One secret of the sweetness of the canary's song may be his freedom from tainted thoughts. Your character beautifies or mars your voice. As a man thinketh in his heart so is his voice.

□

14

Distinctness and Precision of Utterance

In man speaks God.
—**HESIOD**, *Words and Days*

And endless are the modes of speech, and
far Extends from side to side the field of words.
—**HOMER**, *Iliad*

In popular usage the terms "pronunciation," "enunciation," and "articulation" are synonymous, but real pronunciation includes three distinct processes, and may therefore be defined as, *the utterance of a syllable or a group of syllables with regard to articulation, accentuation, and enunciation.*

Distinct and precise utterance is one of the most important considerations of public speech. How preposterous it is to hear a speaker making sounds of "inarticulate earnestness" under the contented delusion that he is telling something to his audience! Telling? Telling means communicating, and how can he actually communicate without making every word distinct?

Slovenly pronunciation results from either physical deformity or habit. A surgeon or a surgeon dentist may correct a deformity, but your own will, working by self-observation and resolution in drill, will break a habit. All depends upon whether you think it worth while.

Defective speech is so widespread that freedom from it is the exception. It is painfully common to hear public speakers mutilate the king's English. If they do not actually murder it, as Curran once said, they often knock an *i* out.

It is insufferable effrontery for any man to appear before an audience who persists in driving the *h* out of happiness, home and heaven, and, to paraphrase Waldo Messaros, will not let it rest in hell. He who does not show enough self-knowledge to see in himself such glaring faults, nor enough self-mastery to correct them, has no business to instruct others. If he *can* do no better, he should be silent. If he *will* do no better, he should also be silent.

Barring incurable physical defects, and few are incurable nowadays, the whole matter is one of will. The catalogue of those who have done the impossible by faithful work is as inspiring as a roll-call of warriors. "The less there is of you," says Nathan Sheppard, "the more need for you to make the most of what there is of you."

Articulation

Articulation is the forming and joining of the elementary sounds of speech. It seems an appalling task to utter articulately the third-of-a million words that go to make up our English vocabulary, but the way to make a beginning is really simple: *learn to utter correctly, and with easy change from one to the other, each of the forty-four elementary sounds in our language.*

The reasons why articulation is so painfully slurred by a great many public speakers are four: ignorance of the elemental sounds; failure to discriminate between sounds nearly alike; a slovenly, lazy use of the vocal organs; and a torpid will. Anyone who is still master of himself will know how to handle each of these defects.

The vowel sounds are the most vexing source of errors,

especially where diphthongs are found.

Bad articulation is frequently the result of joining sounds that do not belong together. For example, no one finds it difficult to say *beauty,* but many persist in pronouncing *duty* as though it were spelled either *dooty* or *juty*. It is not only from untaught speakers that we hear such slovenly articulations as *colyum* for *column,* and *pritty* for *pretty,* but even great orators occasionally offend quite as unblushingly as less noted mortals.

Nearly all such are errors of carelessness, not of pure ignorance, of carelessness because the ear never tries to hear what the lips articulate. It must be exasperating to a foreigner to find that the elemental sound *ou* gives him no hint for the pronunciation of *bough, cough, rough, thorough,* and *through,* and we can well forgive even a man of culture who occasionally loses his way amidst the intricacies of English articulation, but there can be no excuse for the slovenly utterance of the simple vowel sounds which form at once the life and the beauty of our language. He who is too lazy to speak distinctly should hold his tongue.

The consonant sounds occasion serious trouble only for those who do not look with care at the spelling of words about to be pronounced. Nothing but carelessness can account for saying *Jacop, Babtist, sevem, alwus,* or *sadisfy*.

Accentuation

Accentuation is the stressing of the proper syllables in words. This it is that is popularly called *pronunciation*. For instance, we properly say that a word is mispronounced when it is accented *in'-vite* instead of *in-vite'*, though it is really an offence against only one form of pronunciation, accentuation.

It is the work of a lifetime to learn the accents of a large vocabulary and to keep pace with changing usage; but an alert ear, the study of word-origins, and the dictionary habit, will prove to be mighty helpers in a task that can never be finally completed.

Enunciation

Correct enunciation is the complete utterance of all the sounds of a syllable or a word. Wrong articulation gives the wrong sound to the vowel or vowels of a word or a syllable, as *doo* for *dew*; or unites two sounds improperly, as *hully* for *wholly*. Wrong enunciation is the *incomplete* utterance of a syllable or a word, the sound omitted or added being usually consonantal. To say *needcessity* instead of *necessity* is a wrong articulation; to say *doin* for *doing* is improper enunciation. The one articulates, that is, joints, two sounds that should not be joined, and thus gives the word a positively wrong sound; the other fails to touch all the sounds in the word, and *in that particular way* also sounds the word incorrectly.

This slovenly dropping of essential sounds is as offensive as the common habit of running words together so that they lose their individuality and distinctness. *Lighten dark, uppen down, doncher know, partic'lar, zamination,* are all too common to need comment.

Imperfect enunciation is due to lack of attention and to lazy lips. It can be corrected by resolutely attending to the formation of syllables as they are uttered. Flexible lips will enunciate difficult combinations of sounds without slighting any of them, but such flexibility cannot be attained except by habitually uttering words with distinctness and accuracy. A daily exercise in enunciating a series of sounds will in a short time give flexibility to the lips and alertness to the mind, so that no word will be uttered without receiving its due complement of sound.

Returning to our definition, we see that when the sounds of a word are properly articulated, the right syllables accented, and full value given to each sound in its enunciation, we have correct pronunciation. Perhaps one word of caution is needed here, lest any one, anxious to bring out clearly every sound, should overdo the matter and neglect the unity and smoothness of pronunciation. Be careful not to bring syllables into so much prominence as to make words seem long and angular. The joints must be kept decently dressed.

Before delivery, do not fail to go over your manuscript and note every sound that may possibly be mispronounced. Consult the dictionary and make assurance doubly sure. If the arrangement of words is unfavourable to clear enunciation, change either words or order and do not rest until you can follow Hamlet's directions to the players.

□

15

The Truth about Gesture

> When Whitefield acted an old blind man advancing by slow steps towards the edge of the precipice, Lord Chesterfield started up and cried: "Good God, he is gone!"
>
> —NATHAN SHEPPARD
> *Before an Audience*

Gesture is really a simple matter that requires observation and common sense rather than a book of rules. Gesture is an outward expression of an inward condition. It is merely an effect, the effect of a mental or an emotional impulse struggling for expression through physical avenues.

You must not, however, begin at the wrong end: if you are troubled by your gestures, or a lack of gestures, attend to the cause, not the effect. It will not in the least help matters to tack on to your delivery a few mechanical movements. If the tree in your front yard is not growing to suit you, fertilise and water the soil and let the tree have sunshine. Obviously it will not help your tree to nail on a few branches. If your cistern is dry, wait until it rains; or bore a well. Why plunge a pump into a dry hole?

The speaker whose thoughts and emotions are welling within him like a mountain spring will not have much trouble to make gestures; it will be merely a question of properly directing them. If his enthusiasm for his subject is not such as to give him a natural impulse for dramatic action, it will avail nothing to furnish him with a long list of rules. He may tack on some movements, but they will look like the wilted branches nailed to a tree to simulate life. Gestures must be born, not built. A wooden horse may amuse the children, but it takes a live one to go somewhere.

It is not only impossible to lay down definite rules on this subject, but it would be silly to try, for everything depends on the speech, the occasion, the personality and feelings of the speaker, and the attitude of the audience. It is easy enough to forecast the result of multiplying seven by six, but it is impossible to tell any man what kind of gestures he will be impelled to use when he wishes to show his earnestness. We may tell him that many speakers close the hand, with the exception of the forefinger, and pointing that finger straight at the audience pour out their thoughts like a volley; or that others stamp one foot for emphasis; or that Bryan often slaps his hands together for great force, holding one palm upwards in an easy manner; or that Gladstone would sometimes make a rush at the clerk's table in Parliament and smite it with his hand so forcefully that d'israeli once brought down the house by grimly congratulating himself that such a barrier stood between himself and "the honourable gentleman."

All these things, and more, may we tell the speaker, but we cannot know whether he can use these gestures or not, any more than we can decide whether he could wear Bryan's clothes. The best that can be done on this subject is to offer a few practical suggestions, and let personal good taste decide as to where effective dramatic action ends and extravagant motion begins.

Any Gesture That Merely Calls Attention to Itself Is Bad

The purpose of a gesture is to carry your thought and feeling into the minds and hearts of your listeners; this it does by emphasizing your message, by interpreting it, by expressing it in action, by striking its tone in either a physically descriptive, a suggestive, or a typical gesture, and let it be remembered all the time that gesture includes *all* physical movement, from facial expression and the tossing of the head to the expressive movements of hand and foot. A shifting of the pose may be a most effective gesture.

What is true of gesture is true of all life. If the people on the street turn around and watch your walk, your walk is more important than you are, change it. If the attention of your audience is called to your gestures, they are not convincing, because they *appear* to be, what they have a doubtful right to be in reality, studied. Have you ever seen a speaker use such grotesque gesticulations that you were fascinated by their frenzy of oddity, but could not follow his thought? Do not smother ideas with gymnastics.

Only when gesture is subordinated to the absorbing importance of the idea, a spontaneous, living expression of living truth, is it justifiable at all; and when it is remembered for itself, as a piece of unusual physical energy or as a poem of grace, it is a dead failure as dramatic expression. There is a place for a unique style of walking, it is the circus or the cake-walk; there is a place for surprisingly rhythmical evolutions of arms and legs, it is on the dance floor or the stage. Don't let your agility and grace put your thoughts out of business.

Remember, whenever a pair of shoes, a method of pronunciation, or a gesture calls attention to itself, it is bad. When you have made really good gestures in a good speech your listeners will not go away saying, "What beautiful gestures he made!" but they will say, "I'll vote for that measure." "He is right, I believe in that."

Gestures Should Be Born of the Moment

The best actors and public speakers rarely know in advance what gestures they are going to make. They make one gesture on certain words tonight, and none at all tomorrow night at the same point, their various moods and interpretations govern their gestures. It is all a matter of impulse and intelligent feeling with them, don't overlook that word *intelligent*. Nature does not always provide the same kind of sunsets or snow flakes, and the movements of a good speaker vary almost as much as the creations of Nature.

Now all this is not to say that you must not take some thought for your gestures. If that were meant, why this chapter? When the sergeant despairingly besought the recruit in the awkward squad to step out and look at himself, he gave splendid advice, and worthy of personal application. Particularly while you are in the learning days of public speaking you must learn to criticise your own gestures. Recall them, see where they were useless, crude, awkward, what not, and do better next time. There is a vast deal of difference between being conscious of self and being self-conscious.

It will require your nice discrimination in order to cultivate spontaneous gestures and yet give due attention to practice.What spontaneity initiates let practice complete. Every effective speaker and every vivid actor has observed, considered and practiced gesture until his dramatic actions are a sub-conscious possession, just like his ability to pronounce correctly without especially concentrating his thought. Every able platform man has possessed himself of a dozen ways in which he might depict in gesture any given emotion; in fact, the means for such expression are endless, and this is precisely why it is both useless and harmful to make a chart of gestures and enforce them as the ideals of what may be used to express this or that feeling. Practice descriptive, suggestive, and typical movements until they come as naturally as a good articulation; and rarely forecast the gestures you will use at a given moment: leave something to that moment.

Avoid Monotony in Gesture

Roast meat is an excellent dish, but it would be terrible as an exclusive diet. No matter how effective one gesture is, do not overwork it. Put variety in your actions. Monotony will destroy all beauty and power. The pump handle makes one effective gesture, and on hot days that one is very eloquent, but it has its limitations.

Any Movement that is not Significant, Weakens

Do not forget that. Restlessness is not expression. A great many useless movements will only take the attention of the audience from what you are saying. We naturally watch moving objects. A janitor putting down a window can take the attention of the listeners from Roosevelt. By making a few movements at one side of the stage a chorus girl may draw the interest of the spectators from a big scene between the "leads." When our forefathers lived in caves they had to watch moving objects, for movements meant danger. We have not yet overcome the habit. Advertisers have taken advantage of it, witness the moving electric light signs in any city. A shrewd speaker will respect this law and conserve the attention of his audience by eliminating all unnecessary movements.

Gesture Should either be Simultaneous with or Precede the Words, not Follow Them

Lady Macbeth says: "Bear welcome in your eye, your hand, your tongue." Reverse this order and you get comedy. Say, "There he goes," pointing at him after you have finished your words, and see if the result is not comical.

Do Not Make Short, Jerky Movements

Some speakers seem to be imitating a waiter who has failed to get a tip. Let your movements be easy, and from the shoulder, as a rule, rather than from the elbow. But do not go to the other extreme and make too many flowing motions, that savours of the lackadaisical.

Put a little "punch" and life into your gestures. You cannot, however, do this mechanically. The audience will detect it if you do. They may not know just what is wrong, but the gesture will have a false appearance to them.

Facial Expression is Important

Have you ever stopped in front of a theatre and looked at the photographs of the cast? Notice the row of chorus girls who are supposed to be expressing fear. Their attitudes are so mechanical that the attempt is ridiculous. Notice the picture of the "star" expressing the same emotion: his muscles are drawn, his eyebrows lifted, he shrinks, and fear shines through his eyes. That actor *felt* fear when the photograph was taken. The chorus girls felt that it was time for a rarebit, and more nearly expressed that emotion than they did fear. Incidentally, that is one reason why they *stay* in the chorus.

The movements of the facial muscles may mean a great deal more than the movements of the hand. The man who sits in a dejected heap with a look of despair on his face is expressing his thoughts and feelings just as effectively as the man who is waving his arms and shouting from the back of a horse-drawn wagon. The eye has been called the window of the soul. Through it shines the light of our thoughts and feelings.

Do Not Use Too Much Gesture

As a matter of fact, in the big crises of life we do not go through many actions. When your closest friend dies you do not throw up your hands and talk about your grief. You are more likely to sit and brood in dry-eyed silence. Do not fear the man who waves his arms and shouts his anger, but the man who comes up quietly with eyes flaming and face burning may knock you down. Fuss is not force. Observe these principles in Nature and practice them in your delivery.

Posture

The physical attitude to be taken before the audience really is included in gesture. Just what that attitude should be depends, not on rules, but on the spirit of the speech and the occasion. Senator La Follette stood for three hours with his weight thrown on his forward foot as he leaned out over the footlights, ran his fingers through his hair, and flamed out a denunciation of the trusts. It was very effective. But imagine a speaker taking that kind of position to discourse on the development of road-making machinery. If you have a fiery, aggressive message, and will let yourself go, Nature will naturally pull your weight to your forward foot. A man in a hot political argument or a street brawl never has to stop to think upon which foot he should throw his weight. You may sometimes place your weight on your back foot if you have a restful and calm message, but don't worry about it: just stand like a man who genuinely feels what he is saying. Do not stand with your heels close together, like a soldier or a butler. No more should you stand with them wide apart like a traffic policeman. Use simple good manners and common sense.

Here a word of caution is needed. We have advised you to allow your gestures and postures to be spontaneous and not woodenly prepared beforehand, but do not go to the extreme of ignoring the importance of acquiring mastery of your physical movements. A muscular hand made flexible by free movement, is far more likely to be an effective instrument in gesture than a stiff, podgy bunch of fingers. If your shoulders are lithe and carried well, while your chest does not retreat from association with your chin, the chances of using good extemporaneous gestures are so much the better. Learn to keep the *back* of your neck touching your collar, hold your chest high, and keep down your waist measure.

So attention to strength, poise, flexibility, and grace of body are the foundations of good gesture, for they are expressions of vitality, and without vitality no speaker can enter the kingdom of power. When an awkward giant like Abraham Lincoln rose to the sublimest heights of oratory he did so because of the greatness of his soul, his very ruggedness of spirit and artless honesty were properly expressed in his gnarly body. The fire of character, of earnestness, and of message swept his listeners before him when the tepid words of an insincere Apollo would have left no effect. But be sure you are a second Lincoln before you despise the handicap of physical awkwardness.

"If you would learn to stand well before an audience, look at yourself in a mirror, but not too often. Practice walking and standing before the mirror so as to conquer awkwardness, not to cultivate a pose. Stand on the platform in the same easy manner that you would use before guests in a drawing-room. If your position is not graceful, make it so by dancing, gymnasium work, and *by getting grace and poise in your mind*".

Do not continually hold the same position. Any big change of thought necessitates a change of position. Be at home. There are no rules, it is all a matter of taste. While on the platform forget that you have any hands until you desire to use them, then remember them effectively. Gravity will take care of them. Of course, if you want to put them behind you, or fold them once in awhile, it is not going to ruin your speech. Thought and feeling are the big things in speaking, not the position of a foot or a hand. Simply *put* your limbs where you want them to be, you have a will, so do not neglect to use it.

Let us reiterate, do not despise practice. Your gestures and movements may be spontaneous and still be wrong. No matter how natural they are, it is possible to improve them.

It is impossible for anyone, even yourself, to criticise your gestures until after they are made. You can't prune a peach tree until it comes up; therefore speak much, and observe your own speech. While you are examining yourself, do not forget to study statuary and paintings to see how the great portrayers of nature have made their subjects express ideas through action. Notice the gestures of the best speakers and actors. Observe the physical expression of life everywhere. The leaves on the tree respond to the slightest breeze. The muscles of your face, the light of your eyes, should respond to the slightest change of feeling. Emerson says: "Every man that I meet is my superior in some way. In that I learn of him." Open your eyes. Emerson says again: "We are immersed in beauty, but our eyes have no clear vision." Toss this book to one side; go out and watch one child plead with another for a bite of apple; see a street brawl; observe life in action. Do you want to know how to express victory? Watch the victors' hands go high on election night. Do you want to plead a cause? Make a composite photograph of all the pleaders in daily life you constantly see. Beg, borrow, and steal the best you can get, *BUT DON'T GIVE IT OUT AS THEFT*. Assimilate it until it becomes a part of you, then *let* the expression come out.

□

16

Methods of Delivery

The crown, the consummation, of the discourse is its delivery. Toward it all preparation looks, for it the audience waits, by it the speaker is judged.... All the forces of the orator's life converge in his oratory. The logical acuteness with which he marshals the facts around his theme, the rhetorical facility with which he orders his language, the control to which he has attained in the use of his body as a single organ of expression, whatever richness of acquisition and experience are his, these all are now incidents; *the fact is* the sending of his message home to his hearers.... The hour of delivery is the "supreme, inevitable hour" for the orator. It is this fact that makes lack of adequate preparation such an impertinence. And it is this that sends such thrills of indescribable joy through the orator's whole being when he has achieved a success, it is like the mother forgetting her pangs for the joy of bringing a son into the world.

—**J.B.E.**, *How to Attract and Hold an Audience*

There are four fundamental methods of delivering an address; all others are modifications of one or more of these: reading from manuscript, committing the written speech and speaking from memory, speaking from notes, and extemporaneous speech. It is impossible to say which form of delivery is best for all speakers in all circumstances, in deciding for yourself you should consider the occasion, the nature of the audience, the character of your subject, and your own limitations of time and ability. However, it is worthwhile warning you not to be lenient in self-exaction. Say to yourself courageously: What others can do, I can attempt. A bold spirit conquers where others flinch, and a trying task challenges pluck.

Reading from Manuscript

This method really deserves short shrift in a book on public speaking, for, delude yourself as you may, public reading is not public speaking. Yet there are so many who grasp this broken reed for support that we must here discuss the "read speech", apologetic misnomer as it is.

Certainly there are occasions, among them, the opening of Parliament, the presentation of a sore question before a deliberative body, or a historical commemoration, when it may seem not alone to the "orator" but to all those interested that the chief thing is to express certain thoughts in precise language, in language that *must* not be either misunderstood or misquoted. At such times oratory is unhappily elbowed to a back bench, the manuscript is solemnly withdrawn from the capacious inner pocket of the new coat, and everyone settles himself resignedly, with only a feeble flicker of hope that the so-called speech may not be as long as it is thick. The words may be golden, but the listeners' (?) eyes are prone to be leaden, and in about one instance out of a hundred does the perpetrator really deliver an impressive address. His excuse is his apology, he is not to be blamed, as a rule, for someone decreed that it would be dangerous to cut loose from manuscript moorings and take his audience with him on a really delightful sail.

One great trouble on such "great occasions" is that the essayist, for such he is, has been chosen not because of his speaking ability but because his grandfather fought in a certain battle, or his constituents sent him to Parliament, or his gifts in some line of endeavour other than speaking have distinguished him.

It always interests an audience to see a great man; because of his eminence they are likely to listen to his words with respect, perhaps with interest, even when droned from a manuscript. But how much more effective such a deliverance would be if the papers were cast aside!

There are just four motives that can move a man to read his address.

1. Laziness is the commonest. Enough said. Even Heaven cannot make a lazy man efficient.
2. A memory so defective that he really cannot speak without reading. Alas, he is not speaking when he is reading, so his dilemma is painful, and not to himself alone. But no man has a right to assume that his memory is utterly bad until he has buckled down to memory culture, and failed. A weak memory is oftener an excuse than a reason.
3. A genuine lack of time to do more than write the speech. There are such instances, but they do not occur every week! The disposition of your time allows more flexibility than you realize. Motive 3 too often harnesses up with Motive 1.
4. A conviction that the speech is too important to risk forsaking the manuscript. But, if it is vital that every word should be so precise, the style so polished, and the thoughts so logical, that the preacher must write the sermon entire, is not the message important enough to warrant extra effort in perfecting its delivery? It is an insult to a congregation and disrespectful to Almighty God to put the phrasing of a message above the message itself. To reach the hearts

of the listeners the sermon must be delivered, it is only half delivered when the speaker cannot utter it with original fire and force, when he merely repeats words that were conceived hours or weeks before and hence are like champagne that has lost its fizz. The reading preacher's eyes are tied down to his manuscript; he cannot give the audience the benefit of his expression. How long would a play fill a theatre if the actors held their cue-books in hand and read their parts? Imagine Napoleon, constantly looking at his papers, addressing the army at the Pyramids; or Jesus reading the Sermon on the Mount! These speakers were so full of their subjects, their general preparation had been so richly adequate, that there was no necessity for a manuscript, either to refer to or to serve as "an outward and visible sign" of their preparedness. No event was ever so dignified that it required an *artificial* attempt at speech making. Call an essay by its right name, but never call it a speech. Perhaps the most dignified of events is a supplication to the Creator. If you ever listened to the reading of an original prayer you must have felt its superficiality.

Regardless of what the theories may be about manuscript delivery, the fact remains that it does not work out with efficiency. *Avoid it whenever at all possible.*

Committing the Written Speech and Speaking from Memory

This method has certain points in its favour. If you have time and leisure, it is possible to polish and rewrite your ideas until they are expressed in clear, concise terms. Although you cannot devote such painstaking preparation to a speech, you should take time to eliminate useless words, crowd whole paragraphs into a sentence and choose proper illustrations. Good speeches, like plays, are not written; they are rewritten.

The method of writing and committing has been adopted by many noted speakers; Julius Caesar, Robert Ingersoll, and, on some occasions, Wendell Phillips, were distinguished examples. The wonderful effects achieved by famous actors were, of course, accomplished through the delivery of memorised lines.

The inexperienced speaker must be warned before attempting this method of delivery that it is difficult and trying. It requires much skill to make it efficient. The memorised lines of the young speaker will usually *sound* like memorised words, and repel.

If you want to hear an example, listen to a department store demonstrator repeat her memorised lingo about the newest furniture polish or breakfast food. It requires training to make a memorised speech sound fresh and spontaneous, and, unless you have a fine native memory, in each instance the finished product necessitates much labour. Should you forget a part of your speech or miss a few words, you are liable to be so confused that, you will be compelled to repeat your lines from the beginning.

On the other hand, you may be so taken up with trying to recall your written words that you will not abandon yourself to the spirit of your address, and so fail to deliver it with that spontaneity which is so vital to forceful delivery.

But do not let these difficulties frighten you. If committing seems best to you, give it a faithful trial. Do not be deterred by its pitfalls, but by resolute practice avoid them.

One of the best ways to rise superior to these difficulties is to commit without writing the speech, making practically all the preparation mentally, without putting pen to paper, a laborious but effective way of cultivating both mind and memory.

Speaking from Notes

The third, and the most popular method of delivery, is probably also the best one for the beginner. Speaking from notes is not ideal delivery, but we learn to swim in shallow water before going out beyond the ropes.

Make a definite plan for your discourse (for a fuller discussion see Chapter 18) and set down the points somewhat in the fashion of a lawyer's brief, or a preacher's outline. Here is a sample of very simple notes:

Attention

I. Introduction.

Attention indispensable to the performance of any great work. *Anecdote.*

II. Defined and Illustrated.

1. From common observation.
2. From the lives of great men

III. Its Relation to other Mental Powers.

1. Reason.
2. Imagination.
3. Memory.
4. Will. *Anecdote.*

IV. Attention may be Cultivated.

1. Involuntary attention.
2. Voluntary attention. *Examples.*

V. Conclusion.

The consequences of inattention and of attention.

Few briefs would be so precise as this one, for with experience a speaker learns to use little tricks to attract his eye, he may underscore a catch-word heavily, draw a red circle around a pivotal idea, enclose the key-word of an anecdote in a wavy-lined box, and so on indefinitely. These points are worth-remembering, for nothing so eludes the swift-glancing eye of the speaker as the sameness of typewriting, or even a regular pen-script. So unintentional a thing as a blot on the page may help you to remember a big "point" in your brief, perhaps by association of ideas.

An inexperienced speaker would probably require fuller notes than the specimen given. Yet that way lies danger, for the complete manuscript is but a short remove from the copious outline. Use as few notes as possible.

They may be necessary for the time being, but do not fail to look upon them as a necessary evil; and even when you lay them before you, refer to them only when compelled to do so. Make your notes as full as you please in preparation, but by all means condense them for platform use.

Extemporaneous Speech

Surely this is the ideal method of delivery. It is far and away the most popular with the audience, and the favourite method of the most efficient speakers.

"Extemporaneous speech" has sometimes been made to mean unprepared speech, and indeed it is too often precisely that; but in no such sense do we recommend it strongly to speakers old and young. On the contrary, to speak well without notes requires all the preparation which we discussed so fully in the chapter on "Fluency," while yet relying upon the "inspiration of the hour" for some of your thoughts and much of your language. You had better remember, however, that the most effective inspiration of the hour is the inspiration you yourself bring to it, bottled up in your spirit and ready to infuse itself into the audience.

If you extemporise, you can get much closer to your audience. In a sense, they appreciate the task you have before you and send out their sympathy. Extemporise, and you will not have to stop and fumble around amidst your notes, you can keep your eye afire with your message and hold your audience with your very glance. You yourself will feel their response as you read the effects of your warm, spontaneous words, written on their countenances.

Sentences written out in the study are liable to be dead and cold when resurrected before the audience. When you create as you speak you conserve all the native fire of your thought. You can enlarge on one point or omit another, just as the occasion or the mood of the audience may demand. It is not possible for every speaker to use this, the most difficult of all methods of delivery, and least of all can it be used successfully without much practise, but it is the ideal towards which all should strive.

One danger in this method is that you may be led aside from your subject into by-paths. To avoid this peril, firmly stick to your mental outline. Practice speaking from a memorised brief until you gain control. Join a debating society, talk, *talk*, *TALK*, and always extemporise. You may "make a fool of yourself" once or twice, but is that too great a price to pay for success?

Notes, like crutches, are only a sign of weakness. Remember that the power of your speech depends to some extent upon the view your audience holds of you. If you would appear in the light of an authority, be one. Make notes on your brain instead of on paper.

Joint Methods of Delivery

A modification of the second method has been adopted by many great speakers, particularly lecturers who are compelled to speak on a wide variety of subjects day after day; such speakers often commit their addresses to memory but keep their manuscripts in flexible book form before them, turning several pages at a time. They feel safer for having a sheet-anchor to but it is an anchor, nevertheless, and hinders rapid, free sailing.

Other speakers throw out a still lighter anchor by keeping before them a rather full outline of their written and committed speech.

Others again write and commit a few important parts of the address, the introduction, the conclusion, some vital argument, some pat illustration, and depend on the hour for the language of the rest. This method is well adapted to speaking either with or without notes.

Some speakers read from manuscript the most important

parts of their speeches and utter the rest extemporaneously.

Thus, what we have called "joint methods of delivery" are open to much personal variation. You must decide for yourself which is best for you, for the occasion, for your subject, for your audience, for these four factors all have their individual claims.

Whatever form you choose, do not be so weakly indifferent as to prefer the easy way, choose the *best* way, whatever it cost you in time and effort. And of this be assured: only the practiced speaker can hope to gain *both* conciseness of argument and conviction in manner, polish of language and power in delivery, finish of style and fire in utterance.

□

17

Thought and Reserve Power

Providence is always on the side of the last reserve.

—**NAPOLEON BONAPARTE**

So mightiest powers by deepest calms are fed,
And sleep, how oft, in things that gentlest be!

—**BARRY CORNWALL**, *The Sea in Calm*

What would happen if you should overdraw your bank account? As a rule the cheque would be protested; but if you were on friendly terms with the bank, your check might be honoured, and you would be called upon to make good the overdraft.

Nature has no such favourites, therefore extends no credits. She is as relentless as a fuel tank, when the "gas" is all used the machine stops. It is as reckless for a speaker to risk going before an audience without having something in reserve as it is for the motorist to essay a long journey in the wilds without enough gasoline in sight.

But in what does a speaker's reserve power consist? In a well-founded reliance on his general and particular grasp of his subject; in the quality of being alert and resourceful in thought, particularly in the ability to think while on his feet;

and in that self-possession which makes one the captain of all his own forces, bodily and mental.

The first of these elements, adequate preparation, and the last, self-reliance, were discussed fully in the chapters on "Self-Confidence" and "Fluency," so they will be touched only incidentally here; besides, the next chapter will take up specific methods of preparation for public speaking. Therefore the central theme of this chapter is the second of the elements of reserve power, Thought.

The Mental Storehouse

An empty mind, like an empty larder, may be a serious matter or not, all will depend on the available resources. If there is no food in the cupboard the housewife does not nervously rattle the empty dishes; she telephones the grocer. If you have no ideas, do not rattle your empty *ers* and *ahs*, but *get* some ideas, and don't speak until you do get them.

The real solution of the problem of what to do with an empty head is never to let it become empty. In the artesian wells the water rushes to the surface and leaps a score of feet above the ground. The secret of this exuberant flow is of course the great supply below, crowding to get out.

What is the use of stopping to prime a mental pump when you can fill your life with the resources for an artesian well? It is not enough to have merely enough; you must have more than enough. Then the pressure of your mass of thought and feeling will maintain your flow of speech and give you the confidence and poise that denote reserve power. To be away from home with only the exact return fare leaves a great deal to circumstances!

Reserve power is magnetic. It does not consist in giving the idea that you are holding something in reserve, but rather in the suggestion that the audience is getting the cream of your observation, reading, experience, feeling, thought. To have reserve power, therefore, you must have enough milk of material on hand to supply sufficient cream.

But how shall we get the milk? There are two ways: the one is first-hand, from the cow; the other is second-hand, from the milkman.

The Seeing Eye

Some sage has said: "For a thousand men who can speak, there is only one who can think; for a thousand men who can think, there is only one who can see." To see and to think is to get your milk from your own cow.

When the one man in a million who can see comes along, we call him Master. Instead of saying only one man in a million can see, it would strike nearer the truth to say that none of us sees with perfect understanding more than a fraction of what passes before our eyes, yet this faculty of acute and accurate observation is so important that no man ambitious to lead can neglect it. The next time you are in a car, look at those who sit opposite you and see what you can discover of their habits, occupations, ideals, nationalities, environments, education, and so on. You may not see a great deal the first time, but practice will reveal astonishing results. Transmute every incident of your day into a subject for a speech or an illustration. Translate all that you see into terms of speech. When you can describe all that you have seen in definite words, you are seeing clearly. You are becoming the millionth man.

De Maupassant's description of an author should also fit the public-speaker: "His eye is like a suction pump, absorbing everything; like a pickpocket's hand, always at work. Nothing escapes him. He is constantly collecting material, gathering-up glances, gestures, intentions, everything that goes on in his presence, the slightest look, the least act, the merest trifle." De Maupassant was himself a millionth man, a Master.

"Ruskin took a common rock-crystal and saw hidden within its stolid heart lessons which have not yet ceased to move men's lives. Beecher stood for hours before the window of a jewellery store thinking out analogies between jewels and the souls of men. Gough saw in a single drop of water enough truth wherewith to quench the thirst of five thousand souls. Thoreau sat so still in the shadowy woods that birds and insects came and opened up their secret lives to his eye. Emerson observed the soul of a man so long that at length he could say, 'I cannot hear what you say, for seeing what you are.' Preyer for three years studied the life of his babe and so became an authority upon the child mind. Observation! Most men are blind. There are a thousand times as many hidden truths and undiscovered facts about us to-day as have made discoverers famous, facts waiting for some one to 'pluck out the heart of their mystery.' But so long as men go about the search with eyes that see not, so long will these hidden pearls lie in their shells. Not an orator but who could more effectively point and feather his shafts were he to search nature rather than libraries. Too few can see 'sermons in stones' and books in the 'running brooks,' because they are so used to seeing merely sermons in books and only stones in running brooks. Sir Philip Sidney had a saying, 'Look in thy heart and write;' Massillon explained his astute knowledge of the human heart by saying, 'I learned it by studying myself;' Byron says of John Locke that 'all his knowledge of the human understanding was derived from studying his own mind.' Since multiform nature is all about us, originality ought not to be so rare."

The Thinking Mind

Thinking is doing mental arithmetic with facts. Add this fact to that and you reach a certain conclusion. Subtract this truth from another and you have a definite result. Multiply this fact by another and have a precise product. See how many times this occurrence happens in that space of time, and you have reached a calculable dividend. In thought-processes you perform every known problem of arithmetic and algebra. That is why mathematics is such excellent mental gymnastics. But by the same token, thinking is work. Thinking takes energy. Thinking requires time, and patience, and broad information, and clear headedness. Beyond a miserable little surface-scratching, few people really think at all, only one in a thousand, according to the pundit already quoted. So long as the present system of education prevails and children are taught through the ear rather than through the eye, so long as they are expected to remember thoughts of others rather than think for themselves, this proportion will continue, one man in a million will be able to see, and one in a thousand to think.

But, however thoughtless a mind has been, there is promise of better things so soon as the mind detects its own lack of thought-power. The first step is to stop regarding thought as "the magic of the mind," to use Byron's expression, and see it as thought truly is, *a weighing of ideas and a placing of them in relationships to each other*. Ponder this definition and see if you have learned to think efficiently.

Habitual thinking is just that, a habit. Habit comes of doing a thing repeatedly. The lower habits are acquired easily, the higher ones require deeper grooves if they are to persist. So we find that the thought-habit comes only with resolute practice; yet no effort will yield richer dividends. Persist in practice, and whereas you have been able to think only an inch-deep into a subject, you will soon find that you can penetrate it a foot.

Perhaps this homely metaphor will suggest how to begin the practice of consecutive thinking, by which we mean *welding a number of separate thought-links into a chain that will hold*. Take one link at a time, see that each naturally belongs with the ones you link to it, and remember that a single missing link means *no chain*.

Thinking is the most fascinating and exhilarating of all mental exercises. Once realize that your opinion on a subject does not represent the choice you have made between what Dr. Cerebrum has written and Professor Cerebellum has said, but is the result of your own earnestly-applied brain-energy, and you will gain a confidence in your ability to speak on that subject that nothing will be able to shake. Your thought will have given you both power and reserve power.

Someone has condensed the relation of thought to knowledge in these pungent, homely lines:

"Don't give me the man who thinks he thinks,
Don't give me the man who thinks he knows,
But give me the man who knows he thinks,
And I have the man who knows he knows!"

Reading As a Stimulus to Thought

No matter how dry the cow, however, nor how poor our ability to milk, there is still the milkman, we can read what others have seen and felt and thought. Often, indeed, such records will kindle within us that pre-essential and vital spark, the *desire* to be a thinker.

It is fashionable just now to decry the value of reading. We read, we are told, to avoid the necessity of thinking for ourselves. Books are for the mentally lazy.

Though this is only a half-truth, the element of truth it contains is large enough to make us pause. Put yourself through a good old soul-searching self-examination, and if reading-from-thought-laziness is one of your sins, confess it. No one can shrive you of it, but yourself. Do penance for it by using your own brains, for it is a transgression that dwarfs the growth of thought and destroys mental freedom. At first the penance will be trying, but at the last you will be glad in it.

Reading should entertain, give information, or stimulate thought. Here, however, we are chiefly concerned with information, and stimulation of thought.

What shall I read for information?

The ample page of knowledge, as Grey tells us, is "rich with the spoils of time," and these are ours for the price of a theatre ticket. You may command Socrates and Marcus Aurelius to sit beside you and discourse of their choicest, hear Lincoln at Gettysburg and Pericles at Athens, storm the Bastile with Hugo, and wander through Paradise with Dante. You may explore darkest Africa with Stanley, penetrate the human heart with Shakespeare, chat with Carlyle about heroes, and delve with the Apostle Paul into the mysteries of faith. The general knowledge and the inspiring ideas that men have collected through ages of toil and experiment are yours for the asking. The Sage of Chelsea was right: "The true university of these days is a collection of books."

To master a worth-while book is to master much else besides; few of us, however, make perfect conquest of a volume without first owning it physically. To read a borrowed book may be a joy, but to assign your own book a place of its own on your own shelves, be they few or many, to love the book and feel of its worn cover, to thumb it over slowly, page by page, to pencil its margins in agreement or in protest, to smile or thrill with its remembered pungencies, no mere book borrower could ever sense all that delight.

The reader who possesses books in this double sense finds also that his books possess him, and the volumes which most firmly grip his life are likely to be those it has cost him some sacrifice to own. These lightly-come-by titles, which Mr. Fatpurse selects, perhaps by proxy, can scarcely play the guide, philosopher and friend in crucial moments as do the books, long coveted, joyously attained, that are welcomed into the lives, and not merely the libraries, of us others who are at once poorer and richer.

So it is scarcely too much to say that of all the many ways in which an owned, a mastered, book is like to a human friend, the truest ways are these: A friend is worth making sacrifices for, both to gain and to keep; and our loves go out most dearly to those into whose inmost lives we have sincerely entered.

When you have not the advantage of the test of time by which to judge books, investigate as thoroughly as possible the authority of the books you read. Much that is printed and passes current is counterfeit. "I read it in a book" is to many a sufficient warranty of truth, but not to the thinker. "What book?" asks the careful mind. "Who wrote it? What does he know about the subject and what right has he to speak on it? Who recognizes him as authority? With what other recognized authorities does he agree or disagree?" Being caught trying to pass counterfeit money, even unintentionally, is an unpleasant situation. Beware lest you circulate spurious coin.

Above all, seek reading that makes you use your own brains. Such reading must be alive with fresh points of view, packed with special knowledge, and deal with subjects of vital interest. Do not confine your reading to what you already know you will agree with. Opposition wakes one up. The other road may be the better, but you will never know it unless you "give it the once over." Do not do all your thinking and investigating in front of given "Q.E.D.'s;" merely assembling reasons to fill in between your theorem and what you want to prove will get you nowhere. Approach each subject with an open mind and, once sure that you have thought it out thoroughly and honestly, have the courage to abide by the decision of your own thought. But don't brag about it afterwards.

No book on public speaking will enable you to discourse on the tariff if you know nothing about the tariff. Knowing more about it than the other man will be your only hope for making the other man listen to you.

Take a group of men discussing a governmental policy of which some one says: "It is socialistic." That will commend the policy to Mr. A., who believes in socialism, but condemn it to Mr. B., who does not. It may be that neither had considered the policy beyond noticing that its surface-colour was socialistic. The chances are, furthermore, that neither Mr. A. nor Mr. B. has a definite idea of what socialism really is, for as Robert Louis Stevenson says, "Man lives not by bread alone but chiefly by catch words." If you are of this group of men, and have observed this proposed government policy, and investigated it, and thought about it, what you have to say cannot fail to command their respect and approval, for you will have shown them that you possess a grasp of your subject and, to adopt an exceedingly expressive bit of slang, *then* some.

□

18

Subject and Preparation

Suit your topics to your strength, And ponder well your subject, and its length; Nor lift your load, before you're quite aware What weight your shoulders will, or will not, bear.

—**BYRON**, *Hints from Horace*

Look to this day, for it is life, the very life of life. In its brief course lie all the verities and realities of your existence: the bliss of growth, the glory of action, the splendour of beauty. For yesterday is already a dream and tomorrow is only a vision; but today, well lived, makes every yesterday a dream of happiness and every tomorrow a vision of hope. Look well, therefore, to this day. Such is the salutation of the dawn.

From the Sanskrit

In the preceding chapter we have seen the influence of "Thought and Reserve Power" on general preparedness for public speech. But preparation consists in something more definite than the cultivation of thought-power, whether from original or from borrowed sources, it involves a *specifically* acquisitive attitude of the whole life. If you would become a full soul you must constantly take in and assimilate, for in that way only may you hope to give out that which is worth the hearing; but do not confuse the acquisition of general information with the mastery of specific knowledge. Information consists of a fact or a group of facts; knowledge is *organised* information, knowledge knows a fact in relation to other facts.

Now the important thing here is that you should set all your faculties to take in the things about you with the particular object of correlating them and storing them for use in public speech. You must hear with the speaker's ear, see with the speaker's eye, and choose books and companions and sights and sounds with the speaker's purpose in view. At the same time, be ready to receive unplanned-for knowledge. One of the fascinating elements in your life as a public speaker will be the conscious growth in power that casual daily experiences bring. If your eyes are alert you will be constantly discovering facts, illustrations, and ideas without having set out in search of them. These all may be turned to account on the platform; even the leaden events of hum-drum daily life may be melted into bullets for future battles.

Conservation of Time in Preparation

But, you say, I have so little time for preparation, my mind must be absorbed by other matters. Daniel Webster never let an opportunity pass to gather material for his speeches. When he was a boy working in a sawmill, he read out of a book in one hand and busied himself at some mechanical task with the other. In youth Patrick Henry roamed the fields and woods in solitude for days at a time unconsciously gathering material and impressions for his later service as a speaker. Dr. Russell H. Conwell, the man who, the late Charles A. Dana said, had addressed more listeners than any living man, used to memorise long passages from Milton while tending the boiling syrup-pans in the silent New England woods at night. The modern employer would discharge a Webster of today for inattention to duty, and doubtless he would be justified, and Patrick Henry seemed only an idle chap even in those easy-going days; but the truth remains: those who take in power and have the purpose to use it efficiently will some day win to the place in which that stored-up power will revolve great wheels of influence.

Napoleon said that quarter hours decide the destinies of nations. How many quarter hours do we let drift by aimlessly! Robert Louis Stevenson conserved *all his time; every* experience became capital for his work, for capital may be defined as "the results of labour stored up to assist future production." He continually tried to put into suitable language the scenes and actions that were in evidence about him. Emerson says: "Tomorrow will be like today. Life wastes itself whilst we are preparing to live."

Why wait for a more convenient season for this broad, general preparation? The fifteen minutes that we spend on the car could be profitably turned into speech-capital.

Procure a cheap edition of modern speeches, and by cutting out a few pages each day, and reading them during the idle minute here and there, note how soon you can make yourself familiar with the world's best speeches. If you do not wish to mutilate your book, take it with you, most of the epoch-making books are now printed in small volumes. The daily waste of natural gas in the Oklahoma fields is equal to ten thousand tons of coal. Only about three per cent of the power of the coal that enters the furnace ever diffuses itself from your electric bulb as light, the other ninety-seven per cent is wasted. Yet these wastes are no larger, nor more to be lamented than the tremendous waste of time which, if conserved would increase the speaker's powers to their *nth* degree. Scientists are making three ears of corn grow where one grew before; efficiency engineers are eliminating useless motions and products from our factories: catch the spirit of the age and apply efficiency to the use of the most valuable asset you possess, time. What do you do mentally with the time you spend in dressing or in shaving? Take some subject and concentrate your energies on it for a week by utilising just the spare moments that would otherwise be wasted. You will be amazed at the result. One passage a day from the Book of Books, one golden ingot from some master mind, one fully-possessed thought of your own might thus be added to the treasury of your life. Do not waste your time in ways that profit you nothing. Fill "the unforgiving minute" with "sixty seconds' worth of distance run" and on the platform you will be immeasurably the gainer.

Let no word of this, however, seem to decry the value of recreation. Nothing is more vital to a worker than rest, yet nothing is so vitiating to the shirker. Be sure that your recreation re-creates. A pause in the midst of labours gathers strength for new effort. The mistake is to pause too long, or to fill your pauses with ideas that make life flabby.

Choosing a Subject

Subject and materials tremendously influence each other.

"This arises from the fact that there are two distinct ways in which a subject may be chosen: by arbitrary choice, or by development from thought and reading."

Arbitrary choice ... of one subject from among a number involves so many important considerations that no speaker ever fails to appreciate the tone of satisfaction in him who triumphantly announces: 'I have a subject!'

'Do give me a subject!' How often the weary school teacher hears that cry. Then a list of themes is suggested, gone over, considered, and, in most instances, rejected, because the teacher can know but imperfectly what is in the pupil's mind. To suggest a subject in this way is like trying to discover the street on which a lost child lives, by naming over a number of streets until one strikes the little one's ear as sounding familiar.

Choice by development is a very different process. It does not ask, What shall I say? It turns the mind in upon itself and asks, What do I think? Thus, the subject may be said to choose itself, for in the process of thought or of reading one theme rises into prominence and becomes a living germ, soon to grow into the discourse. He who has not learned to reflect is not really acquainted with his own thoughts; hence, his thoughts are not productive. Habits of reading and reflection will supply the speaker's mind with an abundance of subjects of which he already knows something from the very reading and reflection which gave birth to his theme. This is not a paradox, but sober truth.

It must be already apparent that the choice of a subject by development savours more of collection than of conscious selection. The subject *'pops into the mind'*. ... In the intellect of the trained thinker it concentrates, by a process which we have seen to be induction, the facts and truths of which he has been reading and thinking. This is most often a gradual process. The scattered ideas may be but vaguely connected at first, but more and more they concentrate and take on a single form until at length one strong idea seems to grasp the soul with irresistible force, and to cry aloud, 'Arise, I am your *theme*! Henceforth, until you transmute me by the alchemy of your inward fire into vital speech, you shall know no rest!' Happy, then, is that speaker, for he has found a subject that grips him.

Of course, experienced speakers use both methods of selection. Even a reading and reflective man is sometimes compelled to hunt for a theme from Dan to Beersheba, and then the task of gathering materials becomes a serious one. But even in such a case there is a sense in which the selection comes by development, because no careful speaker settles upon a theme which does not represent at least some matured thought"[J. Berg Esenwein].

Deciding on the Subject Matter

Even when your theme has been chosen for you by someone else, there remains to you a considerable field for choice of subject matter. The same considerations, in fact, that would govern you in choosing a theme must guide in the selection of the material. Ask yourself, or someone else, such questions as these:

What is the precise nature of the occasion? How large an audience may be expected? From what walks of life do they come? What is their probable attitude toward the theme? Who else will speak? Do I speak first, last, or where, on the programme? What are the other speakers going to talk about? What is the nature of the auditorium? Is there a desk? Could the subject be more effectively handled if somewhat modified? Precisely how much time am I to fill?

It is evident that many speech-misfits of subject, speaker, occasion and place are due to failure to ask just such pertinent questions. *What* should be said, by *whom,* and *in what circumstances,* constitute ninety per cent of efficiency in public address. No matter who asks you, refuse to be a square peg in a round hole.

Questions of Proportion

Proportion in a speech is attained by a nice adjustment of time. How fully you may treat your subject it is not always for you to say. Let ten minutes mean neither nine nor eleven, though better nine than eleven, at all events. You wouldn't steal a man's watch; no more should you steal the time of the succeeding speaker, or that of the audience. There is no need to overstep time-limits if you make your preparation adequate and divide your subject so as to give each thought its due proportion of attention, and no more. Blessed is the man that maketh short speeches, for he shall be invited to speak again.

Another matter of prime importance is, what part of your address demands the most emphasis. This once decided, you will know where to place that pivotal section so as to give it the greatest strategic value, and what degree of preparation must be given to that central thought so that the vital part may not be submerged by non-essentials. Many a speaker has awakened to find that he has burnt up eight minutes of a ten-minute speech in merely getting up steam. That is like spending eighty percent of your building-money on the vestibule of the house.

The same sense of proportion must tell you to stop precisely when you are through, and it is to be hoped that you will discover the arrival of that period before your audience does.

Tapping Original Sources

The surest way to give life to speech-material is to gather your facts at first hand. Your words come with the weight of authority when you can say, "I have examined the employment rolls of every mill in this district and find that thirty-two per cent of the children employed are under the legal age." No citation of authorities can equal that. You must adopt the methods of the reporter and find out the facts underlying your argument or appeal. To do so may prove laborious, but it should not be irksome, for the great world of fact teems with interest, and over and above all is the sense of power that will come to you from original investigation. To see and feel the facts you are discussing will react upon you much more powerfully than if you were to secure the facts at second hand.

Live an active life among people who are doing worth-while things, keep eyes and ears and mind and heart open to absorb truth, and then tell of the things you know, as if you know them. The world will listen, for the world loves nothing so much as real life.

How to Use a Library

Unsuspected treasures lie in the smallest library. Even when the owner has read every last page of his books it is only in rare instances that he has full indexes to all of them, either in his mind or on paper, so as to make available the vast number of varied subjects touched upon or treated in volumes whose titles would never suggest such topics.

For this reason it is a good thing to take an odd hour now and then to browse. Take down one volume after another and look over its table of contents and its index. (It is a reproach to any author of a serious book not to have provided a full index, with cross references). Then glance over the pages, making notes, mental or physical, of material that looks interesting and usable. Most libraries contain volumes that the owner is "going to read some day." A familiarity with even the contents of such books on your own shelves will enable you to refer to them when you want help. Writings read long ago should be treated in the same way, in every chapter some surprise lurks to delight you.

In looking up a subject do not be discouraged if you do not find it indexed or outlined in the table of contents, you are pretty sure to discover some material under a related title.

Suppose you set to work somewhat in this way to gather references on "Thinking:" First you look over your book titles, and there is Schaeffer's "Thinking and Learning to Think." Near it is Kramer's "Talks to Students on the Art of Study", that seems likely to provide some material, and it does. Naturally you think next of your book on psychology, and there is help there. If you have a volume on the human intellect you will have already turned to it. Suddenly you remember your encyclopaedia and your dictionary of quotations, and now material fairly rains upon you; the problem is what *not to* use. In the encyclopaedia you turn to every reference that includes or touches or even suggests "thinking;" and in the dictionary of quotations you do the same. The latter volume you find peculiarly helpful because it suggests several volumes to you that are on your own shelves, you never would have thought to look in them for references on this subject. Even fiction will supply help, but especially books of essays and biography. Be aware of your own resources.

To make a general index to your library does away with the necessity for indexing individual volumes that are not already indexed.

To begin with, keep a note-book by you; or small cards and paper cuttings in your pocket and on your desk will serve as well. The same note-book that records the impressions of your own experiences and thoughts will be enriched by the ideas of others.

To be sure, this note-book habit means labour, but remember that more speeches have been spoiled by half-hearted preparation than by lack of talent. Laziness is an own-brother to over-confidence, and both are your inveterate enemies, though they pretend to be soothing friends.

Conserve your material by indexing every good idea on cards, thus: On the card illustrated above, clippings are indexed by giving the number of the envelope in which they are filed. The envelopes may be of any size desired and kept in any convenient receptacle. On the foregoing example, "Progress of S., Envelope 16," will represent a clipping, filed in Envelope 16, which is, of course, numbered arbitrarily.

The fractions refer to books in your library, the numerator being the book-number, the denominator referring to the page. Thus, "S. a fallacy, 96/210," refers to page 210 of volume 96 in your library. By some arbitrary sign, say red ink, you may even index a reference in a public library book.

If you preserve your magazines, important articles may be indexed by month and year. An entire volume on a subject may be indicated like the imaginary book by "Forbes." If you clip the articles, it is better to index them according to the envelope system.

Your own writings and notes may be filed in envelopes with the clippings or in a separate series.

Another good indexing system combines the library index with the "scrap," or clipping, system by making the outside of the envelope serve the same purpose as the card for the indexing of books, magazines, clippings and manuscripts, the latter two classes of material being enclosed in the envelopes that index them, and all filed alphabetically.

When your cards accumulate so as to make ready reference difficult under a single alphabet, you may subdivide each letter by subordinate guide cards marked by the vowels, A, E, I, O, U. Thus, "Antiquities" would be filed under *i* in A, because A begins the word, and the second letter, *n*, comes after the vowel *i* in the alphabet, but before *o*. In the same manner, "Beecher" would be filed under *e* in B; and "Hydrogen" would come under *u* in H.

Outlining the Address

No one can advise you how to prepare the notes for an address. Some speakers get the best results while walking out and ruminating, jotting down notes as they pause in their walk. Others never put pen to paper until the whole speech has been thought out. The great majority, however, will take notes, classify their notes, write a hasty first draft, and then revise the speech. Try each of these methods and choose the one that is best, *for you*. Do not allow any man to force you to work in *his* way; but do not neglect to consider *his* way, for it may be better than your own.

For those who make notes and with their aid write out the speech, these suggestions may prove helpful:

After having read and thought enough, classify your notes by setting down the big, central thoughts of your material on separate cards or slips of paper. These will stand in the same relation to your subject as chapters do to a book.

Then arrange these main ideas or heads in such an order that they will lead effectively to the result you have in mind, so that the speech may rise in argument, in interest, in power, by piling one fact or appeal upon another until the climax, the highest point of influence on your audience, has been reached.

Next group all your ideas, facts, anecdotes, and illustrations under the foregoing main heads, each where it naturally belongs.

You now have a skeleton or outline of your address that in its polished form might serve either as the brief, or manuscript notes, for the speech or as the guide-outline which you will expand into the written address, if written it is to be.

Imagine each of the main ideas as being separate; then picture your mind as sorting them out and placing them in order; finally, conceive of how you would fill in the facts and examples under each head, giving special prominence to those you wish to emphasize and subduing those of less moment. In the end, you have the outline complete. The simplest form of outline, not very suitable for use on the platform, however, is the following:

Why Prosperity is Coming

What prosperity means., The real tests of prosperity., Its basis in the soil., American agricultural progress., New interest in farming., Enormous value of our agricultural products., Reciprocal effect on trade., Foreign countries affected., Effects of our new internal economy, the regulation of banking and "big business", on prosperity., Effects of our revised attitude toward foreign markets, including our merchant marine., Summary.

Obviously, this very simple outline is capable of considerable expansion under each head by the addition of facts, arguments, inferences and examples.

Writing and Revision

After the outline has been perfected comes the time to write the speech, if write it you must. Then, whatever you do, write it at white heat, with not *too* much thought of anything but the strong, appealing expression of your ideas.

The final stage is the paring down, the re-vision, the seeing again, as the word implies, when all the parts of the speech must be impartially scrutinised for clearness, precision, force, effectiveness, suitability, proportion, logical climax; and in all this you must *imagine yourself to be before your audience*, for a speech is not an essay and what will convince and arouse in the one will not prevail in the other.

The Title

Often last of all will come that which in a sense is first of all, the title, the name by which the speech is known. Sometimes it will be the simple theme of the address, as "The New Americanism," by Henry Watterson; or it may be a bit of symbolism typifying the spirit of the address, as "Acres of Diamonds," by Russell H. Conwell; or it may be a fine phrase taken from the body of the address, as "Pass Prosperity Around," by Albert J. Beveridge. All in all, from whatever motive it be chosen, let the title be fresh, short, suited to the subject, and likely to excite interest.

□

19

Influencing by Exposition

> Speak not at all, in any wise, till you have somewhat to speak; care not for the reward of your speaking, but simply and with undivided mind for the truth of your speaking.
>
> — **THOMAS CARLYLE**
> Essay on *Biography*

A complete discussion of the rhetorical structure of public speeches requires a fuller treatise than can be undertaken in a work of this nature, yet in this chapter, and in the succeeding ones on "Description," "Narration," "Argument," and "Pleading," the underlying principles are given and explained as fully as need be for a working knowledge, and adequate book references are given for those who would perfect themselves in rhetorical art.

The Nature of Exposition

In the word "expose", *to lay bare, to uncover, to show the true inwardness of*, we see the foundation-idea of "Exposition." It is the clear and precise setting forth of what the subject really is, it is explanation.

Exposition does not draw a picture, for that would be description. To tell in exact terms what the automobile is, to name its characteristic parts and explain their workings, would be exposition; so would an explanation of the nature of "fear." But to create a mental image of a particular automobile, with its glistening body, graceful lines, and great speed, would be description; and so would a picturing of fear acting on the emotions of a child at night. Exposition and description often intermingle and overlap, but fundamentally they are distinct. Their differences will be touched upon again in the chapter on "Description."

Exposition furthermore does not include an account of how events happened, that is narration. When Peary lectured on his polar discoveries he explained the instruments used for determining latitude and longitude, that was exposition. In picturing his equipment he used description. In telling of his adventures day by day he employed narration. In supporting some of his contentions he used argument. Yet he mingled all these forms throughout the lecture.

Neither does exposition deal with reasons and inferences, that is the field of argument. A series of connected statements intended to convince a prospective buyer that one automobile is better than another, or proofs that the appeal to fear is a wrong method of discipline, would not be exposition. The plain facts as set forth in expository speaking or writing are nearly always the basis of argument, yet the processes are not one. True, the statement of a single significant fact without the addition of one other word may be convincing, but a moment's thought will show that the inference, which completes a chain of reasoning, is made in the mind of the listeners and presupposes other facts held in consideration.

In like manner, it is obvious that the field of persuasion is not open to exposition, for exposition is entirely an intellectual process, with no emotional element.

The Importance of Exposition

The importance of exposition in public speech is precisely

the importance of setting forth a matter so plainly that it cannot be misunderstood.

"To master the process of exposition is to become a clear thinker. 'I know, when you do not ask me,' replied a gentleman upon being requested to define a highly complex idea. Now some large concepts defy explicit definition; but no mind should take refuge behind such exceptions, for where definition fails, other forms succeed. Sometimes we feel confident that we have perfect mastery of an idea, but when the time comes to express it, the clearness becomes a haze. Exposition, then, is the test of clear understanding. To speak effectively you must be able to see your subject clearly and comprehensively, and to make your audience see it as you do." [J.berg Esenwein]

There are pitfalls on both sides of this path. To explain too little will leave your audience in doubt as to what you mean. It is useless to argue a question if it is not perfectly clear just what is meant by the question. Have you never come to a blind lane in conversation by finding that you were talking of one aspect of a matter while your friend was thinking of another? If two do not agree in their definitions of a Musician, it is useless to dispute over a certain man's right to claim the title.

On the other side of the path lies the abyss of tediously explaining too much. That offends because it impresses the listeners that you either do not respect their intelligence or are trying to blow a breeze into a tornado. Carefully estimate the probable knowledge of your audience, both in general and of the particular point you are explaining. In trying to simplify, it is fatal to "sillify." To explain more than is needed for the purposes of your argument or appeal is to waste energy all around. In your efforts to be explicit do not press exposition to the extent of dullness, the confines are not far distant and you may arrive before you know it.

Some Purposes of Exposition

From what has been said it ought to be clear that, primarily, exposition weaves a cord of understanding between you and your audience. It lays, furthermore, a foundation of fact on which to build later statements, arguments, and appeals. In scientific and purely "information" speeches exposition may exist by itself and for itself, as in a lecture on biology, or on psychology; but in the vast majority of cases it is used to accompany and prepare the way for the other forms of discourse.

Clearness, precision, accuracy, unity, truth, and necessity, these must be the *constant* standards by which you test the efficiency of your expositions, and, indeed, that of every explanatory statement. This dictum should be written on your brain in letters most plain. And let this apply not alone to the *purposes* of exposition but in equal measure to your use of the following :

Methods of Exposition

The various ways along which a speaker may proceed in exposition are likely to touch each other now and then, and even when they do not meet and actually overlap they run so nearly parallel that the roads are sometimes distinct rather in theory than in any more practical respect.

Definition, the primary expository method, is a statement of precise limits. Obviously, here the greatest care must be exercised that the terms of definition should not themselves demand too much definition; that the language should be concise and clear; and that the definition should neither exclude nor include too much. The following is a simple example:

To expound is to set forth the nature, the significance, the characteristics, and the bearing of an idea or a group of ideas.

—**ARLO BATES**, *Talks on Writing English*

Contrast and Antithesis are often used effectively to amplify definition, as in this sentence, which immediately follows the above-cited definition:

Exposition therefore differs from Description in that it deals directly with the meaning or intent of its subject instead of with its appearance.

This antithesis forms an expansion of the definition, and as such it might have been still further extended. In fact, this is a frequent practice in public speech, where the minds of the listeners often ask for reiteration and expanded statement to help them grasp a subject in its several aspects. This is the very heart of exposition, to amplify and clarify all the terms by which a matter is defined.

Example is another method of amplifying a definition or of expounding an idea more fully. The following sentences immediately succeed Bates's definition and contrast just quoted:

A good deal which we are accustomed inexactly to call description is really exposition. Suppose that your small boy wishes to know how an engine works, and should say: "Please describe the steam-engine to me." If you insist on taking his words literally, and are willing to run the risk of his indignation at being wilfully misunderstood, you will to the best of your ability picture to him this familiarly wonderful machine. If you explain it to him, you are not describing but expounding it.

The chief value of example is that it makes clear the unknown by referring the mind to the known. Readiness of mind to make illuminating, apt comparisons for the sake of clearness is one of the speaker's chief resources on the platform, it is the greatest of all teaching gifts. It is a gift, moreover, that responds to cultivation. Read the three extracts from Arlo Bates as their author delivered them, as one passage, and see how they melt into one, each part supplementing the other most helpfully.

Analogy, which calls attention to similar relationships in objects not otherwise similar, is one of the most useful methods of exposition. The following striking specimen is from Beecher's Liverpool speech:

> A savage is a man of one story, and that one story a cellar. When a man begins to be civilised he raises another story. When you Christianize and civilise the man, you put story upon story, for you develop faculty after faculty; and you have to supply every story with your productions.

Discarding is a less common form of platform explanation. It consists in clearing away associated ideas so that the attention may be centered on the main thought to be discussed. Really, it is a negative factor in exposition though a most important one, for it is fundamental to the consideration of an intricately related matter that subordinate and side questions should be set aside in order to bring out the main issue. Here is an example of the method:

I cannot allow myself to be led aside from the only issue before this jury. It is not pertinent to consider that this prisoner is the husband of a heartbroken woman and that his babes will go through the world under the shadow of the law's extremest penalty worked upon their father. We must forget the venerable father and the mother whom Heaven in pity took before she learned of her son's disgrace. What have these matters of heart, what have the blenched faces of his friends, what have the prisoner's long and honourable career to say before this bar when you are sworn to weigh only the direct evidence before you? The one and only question for you to decide on the evidence is whether this man did with revengeful intent commit the murder that every impartial witness has solemnly laid at his door.

Classification assigns a subject to its class. By an allowable extension of the definition it may be said to assign it also to its order, genus, and species. Classification is useful in public speech in narrowing the issue to a desired phase. It is equally valuable for showing a thing in its relation to other things, or in correlation. Classification is closely akin to Definition and Division.

"This question of the liquor traffic, sirs, takes its place beside the grave moral issues of all times. Whatever be its economic significance, and who is there to question it, whatever vital bearing it has upon our political system, and is there one who will deny it?, the question of the licensed saloon must quickly be settled as the world in its advancement has settled the questions of constitutional government for the masses, of the opium traffic, of the serf, and of the slave, not as matters of economic and political expediency but as questions of right and wrong."

Analysis separates a subject into its essential parts. This it may do by various principles; for example, analysis may follow the order of time (geologic eras), order of place (geographic facts), logical order (a sermon outline), order of increasing interest, or procession to a climax (a lecture on 20th century poets); and so on. A classic example of analytical exposition is the following:

"In philosophy the contemplations of man do either penetrate unto God, or are circumferred to Nature, or are reflected or reverted upon himself. Out of which several inquiries there do arise three knowledges: divine philosophy, natural philosophy, and human philosophy or humanity. For all things are marked and stamped with this triple character, of the power of God, the difference of nature, and the use of man."

—**LORD BACON**, *The Advancement of Learning*

Division differs only from analysis in that analysis follows the inherent divisions of a subject, as illustrated in the foregoing passage, while division arbitrarily separates the subject for convenience of treatment, as in the following none-too-logical example:

For civil history, it is of three kinds; not unfittingly to be compared with the three kinds of pictures or images. For of pictures or images, we see some are unfinished, some are perfect, and some are defaced. So of histories we may find three kinds, memorials, perfect histories, and antiquities; for memorials are history unfinished, or the first or rough drafts of history; and antiquities are history defaced, or some remnants of history which have casually escaped the shipwreck of time.

—**LORD BACON**, *The Advancement of Learning*

Generalisation states a broad principle, or a general truth, derived from examination of a considerable number of individual facts. This synthetic exposition is not the same as argumentative generalisation, which supports a general contention by citing instances in proof. Observe how George Holmes begins with one fact, and by adding another and another reaches a complete whole. This is one of the most effective devices in the public speaker's repertory.

"Take a hollow cylinder, the bottom closed while the top remains open, and pour in water to the height of a few inches. Next cover the water with a flat plate or piston, which fits the interior of the cylinder perfectly; then apply heat to the water, and we shall witness the following phenomena. After the lapse of some minutes the water will begin to boil, and the steam accumulating at the upper surface will make room for itself by raising the piston slightly. As the boiling continues, more and more steam will be formed, and raise the piston higher and higher, till all the water is boiled away, and nothing but steam is left in the cylinder. Now this machine, consisting of cylinder, piston, water, and fire, is the steam-engine in its most elementary form. For a steam-engine may be defined as an apparatus for doing work by means of heat applied to water; and since raising such a weight as the piston is a form of doing work, this apparatus, clumsy and inconvenient though it may be, answers the definition precisely" [G.C.V. Holmes].

Reference to Experience is one of the most vital principles in exposition, as in every other form of discourse.

"Reference to experience, as here used, means reference

to the known. The known is that which the listener has seen, heard, read, felt, believed or done, and which still exists in his consciousness, his stock of knowledge. It embraces all those thoughts, feelings and happenings which are to him real. Reference to Experience, then, means *coming into the listener's life*" [ArthurE.Phillips].

The vast results obtained by science are won by no mystical faculties, by no mental processes, other than those which are practised by every one of us in the humblest and meanest affairs of life. A detective policeman discovers a burglar from the marks made by his shoe, by a mental process identical with that by which Cuvier restored the extinct animals of Montmartre from fragments of their bones. Nor does that process of induction and deduction by which a lady, finding a stain of a particular kind upon her dress, concludes that somebody has upset the inkstand thereon, differ in any way from that by which Adams and Leverrier discovered a new planet. The man of science, in fact, simply uses with scrupulous exactness the methods which we all habitually, and at every moment, use carelessly.

—**THOMAS HENRY HUXLEY**, *Lay Sermons*

Do you set down your name in the scroll of youth, that are written down old with all the characters of age? Have you not a moist eye? a dry hand? a yellow cheek? a white beard? a decreasing leg? an increasing belly? is not your voice broken? your wind short? your chin double? your wit single? and every part about you blasted with antiquity? and will you yet call yourself young? Fie, fie, fie, Sir John!

—**SHAKESPEARE**, *The Merry Wives of Windsor*

Finally, in preparing expository material ask yourself these questions regarding your subject:

What is it, and what is it not?

What is it like, and unlike?

What are its causes, and effects?

How shall it be divided?
With what subjects is it correlated?
What experiences does it recall?
What examples illustrate it?

□

20

Influencing by Description

The groves of Eden vanish'd now so long,
Live in description, and look green in song.
—**ALEXANDER POPE**, *Windsor Forest*

The moment our discourse rises above the ground-line of familiar facts, and is inflamed with passion or exalted thought, it clothes itself in images. A man conversing in earnest, if he watch his intellectual processes, will find that always a material image, more or less luminous, arises in his mind, contemporaneous with every thought, which furnishes the vestment of the thought.... This imagery is spontaneous. It is the blending of experience with the present action of the mind. It is proper creation.
—**RALPH WALDO EMERSON**, *Nature*

Like other valuable resources in public speaking, description loses its power when carried to an extreme. Over-ornamentation makes the subject ridiculous. A dust-cloth is a very useful thing, but why embroider it? Whether description shall be restrained within its proper and important limits, or be encouraged to run riot, is the personal choice that comes before every speaker, for man's earliest literary tendency is to depict.

The Nature of Description

To describe is to call up a picture in the mind of the listener. "In talking of description we naturally speak of portraying, delineating, coloruing, and all the devices of the picture painter. To describe is to visualise, hence we must look at description as a pictorial process, whether the writer deals with material or with spiritual objects." [J.Berg Esenwein]

If you were asked to describe the rapid-fire gun you might go about it in either of two ways: give a cold technical account of its mechanism, in whole and in detail, or else describe it as a terrible engine of slaughter, dwelling upon its effects rather than upon its structure.

The former of these processes is exposition, the latter is true description. Exposition deals more with the *general,* while description must deal with the *particular*. Exposition elucidates *ideas,* description treats of *things.* Exposition deals with the *abstract,* description with the *concrete.* Exposition is concerned with the *internal,* description with the *external.* Exposition is *enumerative, description literary.* Exposition is *intellectual,* description *sensory*. Exposition is *impersonal,* description *personal.*

If description is a visualizing process for the listener, it is first of all such for the speaker, he cannot describe what he has never seen, either physically or in fancy. It is this personal quality, this question of the personal eye which sees the things later to be described, that makes description so interesting in public speech. Given a speaker of personality, and we are interested in his personal view, his view adds to the natural interest of the scene, and may even be the sole source of that interest to his audience.

The seeing eye has been praised in an earlier chapter (on "Subject and Preparation") and the imagination will be treated in a subsequent one (on "Riding the Winged Horse"), but here we must consider the *picturing mind*: the mind that forms the double habit of seeing things clearly, for we see more with the mind than we do with the physical eye, and then of re-imaging these things for the purpose of getting them before the minds' eyes of the listeners. No habit is more useful than that of visualizing clearly the object, the scene, the situation, the action, the person, about to be described. Unless that primary process is carried out clearly, the picture will be blurred for the listeners-beholder.

In a work of this nature we are concerned with the rhetorical analysis of description, and with its methods, only so far as may be needed for the practical purposes of the speaker. The following grouping, therefore, will not be regarded as complete, nor will it here be necessary to add more than a word of explanation:

Description for Public Speakers

Objects	{ Still
"	{ In motion
Scenes	{ Still
"	{ Including action
Situations	{ Preceding change
"	{ During change
"	{ After change
Actions	{ Mental
"	{ Physical
Persons	{ Internal
"	{ External

Some of the foregoing processes will overlap, in certain instances, and all are more likely to be found in combination than singly.

When description is intended solely to give accurate information, as to delineate the appearance, not the technical construction, of the latest Zeppelin airship, it is called "scientific description," and is akin to exposition. When it is intended to present a free picture for the purpose of making a vivid impression, it is called "artistic description." With both of these the public speaker has to deal, but more frequently with the latter form. Rhetoricians make still further distinctions.

Methods of Description

In public speaking, *description should be mainly by suggestion,* not only because suggestive description is so much more compact and time-saving but because it is so vivid. Suggestive expressions connote more than they literally say, they suggest ideas and pictures to the mind of the listener which supplement the direct words of the speaker. When Dickens, in his "Christmas Carol," says: "In came Mrs. Fezziwig, one vast substantial smile," our minds complete the picture so deftly begun, a much more effective process than that of a minutely detailed description because it leaves a unified, vivid impression, and that is what we need. Here is a present-day bit of suggestion: "General Trinkle was a gnarly oak of a man, rough, solid, and safe; you always knew where to find him." Dickens presents Miss Peecher as: "A little pin-cushion, a little housewife, a little book, a little work-box, a little set of tables and weights and measures, and a little woman all in one." In his "Knickerbocker's" "History of New York," Irving portrays Wouter van Twiller as "a robustious beer-barrel, standing on skids."

Whatever forms of description you neglect, be sure to master the art of suggestion.

Description may be by simple hint. Lowell notes a happy instance of this sort of picturing by intimation when he says of Chaucer: "Sometimes he describes amply by the merest hint, as where the Friar, before setting himself down, drives away the cat. We know without need of more words that he has chosen the snuggest corner."

Description may depict a thing by its effects. "When the spectator's eye is dazzled, and he shades it," says Mozley in his "Essays," "we form the idea of a splendid object; when his face turns pale, of a horrible one; from his quick wonder and admiration we form the idea of great beauty; from his silent awe, of great majesty."

Brief description may be by epithet. "Blue-eyed," "white-armed," "laughter-loving," are now conventional compounds, but they were fresh enough when Homer first conjoined them. The centuries have not yet improved upon "Wheels round, brazen, eight-spoked," or "Shields smooth, beautiful, brazen, well-hammered." Observe the effective use of epithet in Will Levington Comfort's "The Fighting Death," when he speaks of soldiers in a Philippine skirmish as being "leeched against a rock."

Description uses figures of speech. Any advanced rhetoric will discuss their forms and give examples for guidance. This matter is most important, be assured. A brilliant yet carefully restrained figurative style, a style marked by brief, pungent, witty, and humorous comparisons and characterisations, is a wonderful resource for all kinds of platform work.

Description may be direct. This statement is plain enough without exposition. Use your own judgement as to whether in picturing you had better proceed from a general view to the details, or first give the details and thus build up the general picture, but by all means BE BRIEF.

Note the vivid compactness of these delineations from Washington Irving's "Knickerbocker:"

"He was a short, square, brawny old gentleman, with a double chin, a mastiff mouth, and a broad copper nose, which was supposed in those days to have acquired its fiery hue from the constant neighbourhood of his tobacco pipe".

"He was exactly five feet six inches in height, and six feet five inches in circumference. His head was a perfect sphere, and of such stupendous dimensions, that Dame Nature, with all her sex's ingenuity, would have been puzzled to construct a neck capable of supporting it; wherefore she wisely declined the attempt, and settled it firmly on the top of his backbone, just between the shoulders. His body was of an oblong form, particularly capacious at bottom; which was wisely ordered by Providence, seeing that he was a man of sedentary habits, and very averse to the idle labour of walking".

The foregoing is too long for the platform, but it is so good-humoured, so full of delightful exaggeration, that it may well serve as a model of humorous character picturing, for here one inevitably sees the inner man in the outer.

Direct description for platform use may be made vivid by the *sparing* use of the "historical present." The following dramatic passage, accompanied by the most lively action, has lingered in the mind for thirty years after hearing Dr. T. De Witt Talmage lecture on "Big Blunders." The crack of the bat sounds clear even today:

"Get ready the bats and take your positions. Now, give us the ball. Too low. Don't strike. Too high. Don't strike. There it comes like lightning. Strike! Away it soars! Higher! Higher! Run! Another base! Faster! Faster! Good! All around at one stroke!"

Observe the remarkable way in which the lecturer fused speaker, audience, spectators, and players into one excited, ecstatic whole, just as you have found yourself starting forward in your seat at the delivery of the ball with "three on and two down" in the ninth innings. Notice, too, how, perhaps unconsciously, Talmage painted the scene in Homer's characteristic style: not as having already happened, but as happening before your eyes.

If you have attended many travel talks you must have been impressed by the painful extremes to which the lecturers go, with a few notable exceptions, their language is either over-ornate or crude. If you would learn the power of words to make scenery, yes, even houses, palpitate with poetry and human appeal, read Lafcadio Hearn, Robert Louis Stevenson, Pierre Loti, and Edmondo De Amicis.

Blue-distant, a mountain of carven stone appeared before

them, the Temple, lifting to heaven its wilderness of chiselled pinnacles, flinging to the sky the golden spray of its decoration.

—**LAFCADIO HEARN**, *Chinese Ghosts*

The stars were clear, coloured, and jewel-like, but not frosty. A faint silvery vapour stood for the Milky Way. All around me the black fir-points stood upright and stock-still. By the whiteness of the pack-saddle I could see Modestine walking round and round at the length of her tether; I could hear her steadily munching at the sward; but there was not another sound save the indescribable quiet talk of the runnel over the stones.

—**ROBERT LOUIS STEVENSON**, *Travels with a Donkey*

It was full autumn now, late autumn, with the nightfalls gloomy, and all things growing dark early in the old cottage, and all the Breton land looking sombre, too. The very days seemed but twilight; immeasurable clouds, slowly passing, would suddenly bring darkness at broad noon. The wind moaned constantly, it was like the sound of a great cathedral organ at a distance, but playing profane airs, or despairing dirges; at other times it would come close to the door, and lift up a howl like wild beasts.

—**PIERRE LOTI**, *An Iceland Fisherman*

I see the great refectory, where a battalion might have drilled; I see the long tables, the five hundred heads bent above the plates, the rapid motion of five hundred forks, of a thousand hands, and sixteen thousand teeth; the swarm of servants running here and there, called to, scolded, hurried, on every side at once; I hear the clatter of dishes, the deafening noise, the voices choked with food crying out: "Bread, bread!" and I feel once more the formidable appetite, the herculean strength of jaw, the exuberant life and spirits of those far-off days.

—**EDMONDO DE AMICIS**, *College Friends*

Suggestions for the Use of Description

Decide, on beginning a description, what point of view you wish your listeners to take. One cannot see either a mountain or a man on all sides at once. Establish a viewpoint, and do not shift without giving notice.

Choose an attitude toward your subject—shall it be idealised? caricatured? ridiculed? exaggerated? defended? or described impartially?

Be sure of your mood, too, for it will colour the subject to be described. Melancholy will make a rose-garden look grey.

Adopt an order in which you will proceed—do not shift backwards and forwards from near to far, remote to close in time, general to particular, large to small, important to unimportant, concrete to abstract, physical to mental; but follow your chosen order. Scattered and shifting observations produce hazy impressions just as a moving camera spoils the time-exposure.

Do not go into needless minutiae. Some details identify a thing with its class, while other details differentiate it from its class. Choose only the significant, suggestive characteristics and bring those out with terse vividness. Learn a lesson from the few strokes used by the poster artist.

In determining what to describe and what merely to name, seek to read the knowledge of your audience. The difference to them between the unknown and the known is a vital one also to you.

Relentlessly cut out all ideas and words not necessary to produce the effect you desire. Each element in a mental picture either helps or hinders. Be sure they do not hinder, for they cannot be passively present in any discourse.

Interruptions of the description to make side-remarks are as powerful to destroy unity as are scattered descriptive phrases. The only visual impression that can be effective is one that is unified.

In describing, try to call up the emotions you felt when

first you saw the scene, and then try to reproduce those emotions in your listeners. Description is primarily emotional in its appeal; nothing can be more deadly dull than a cold, unemotional outline, while nothing leaves a warmer impression than a glowing, spirited description.

Give a swift and vivid general view at the close of the portrayal. First and final impressions remain the longest. The mind may be trained to take in the characteristic points of a subject, so as to view in a single scene, action, experience, or character, a unified impression of the whole. To describe a thing as a whole you must first see it as a whole. Master that art and you have mastered description to the last degree.

Selections for Practise ***The Homes of The People***

I went to Washington the other day, and I stood on the Capitol Hill; my heart beat quick as I looked at the towering marble of my country's Capitol and the mist gathered in my eyes as I thought of its tremendous significance, and the armies and the treasury, and the judges and the President, and the Congress and the courts, and all that was gathered there. And I felt that the sun in all its course could not look down on a better sight than that majestic home of a republic that had taught the world its best lessons of liberty. And I felt that if honour and wisdom and justice abided therein, the world would at last owe to that great house in which the ark of the covenant of my country is lodged, its final uplifting and its regeneration.

Two days afterwards, I went to visit a friend in the country, a modest man, with a quiet country home. It was just a simple, unpretentious house, set about with big trees, encircled in meadow and field rich with the promise of harvest. The fragrance of the pink and hollyhock in the front yard was mingled with the aroma of the orchard and of the gardens, and resonant with the cluck of poultry and the hum of bees.

Inside was quiet, cleanliness, thrift, and comfort. There was the old clock that had welcomed, in steady measure, every newcomer to the family, that had ticked the solemn requiem of the dead, and had kept company with the watcher at the bedside. There were the big, restful beds and the old, open fireplace, and the old family Bible, thumbed with the fingers of hands long since still, and wet with the tears of eyes long since closed, holding the simple annals of the family and the heart and the conscience of the home.

Outside, there stood my friend, the master, a simple, upright man, with no mortgage on his roof, no lien on his growing crops, master of his land and master of himself. There was his old father, an aged, trembling man, but happy in the heart and home of his son. And as they started to their home, the hands of the old man went down on the young man's shoulder, laying there the unspeakable blessing of the honoured and grateful father and ennobling it with the knighthood of the fifth commandment.

And as they reached the door the old mother came with the sunset falling fair on her face, and lighting up her deep, patient eyes, while her lips, trembling with the rich music of her heart, bade her husband and son welcome to their home. Beyond was the housewife, busy with her household cares, clean of heart and conscience, the buckler and helpmeet of her husband. Down the lane came the children, trooping home after the cows, seeking as truant birds do the quiet of their home nest.

And I saw the night come down on that house, falling gently as the wings of the unseen dove. And the old man—while a startled bird called from the forest, and the trees were shrill with the cricket's cry, and the stars were swarming in the sky—got the family around him, and, taking the old Bible from the table, called them to their knees, the little baby hiding in the folds of its mother's dress, while he closed the record of that simple day by calling down God's benediction on that family and that home. And while I gazed, the vision of that marble Capitol faded. Forgotten were its treasures and its majesty and I said, "Oh, surely here in the homes of the people are lodged at last the strength and the responsibility of this government, the hope and the promise of this republic."

—HENRY W. GRADY

Suggestive Scenes

One thing in life calls for another; there is a fitness in events and places. The sight of a pleasant arbour puts it in our mind to sit there. One place suggests work, another idleness, a third early rising and long rambles in the dew. The effect of night, of any flowing water, of lighted cities, of the peep of day, of ships, of the open ocean, calls up in the mind an army of anonymous desires and pleasures. Something, we feel, should happen; we know not what, yet we proceed in quest of it. And many of the happiest hours in life fleet by us in this vain attendance on the genius of the place and moment. It is thus that tracts of young fir, and low rocks that reach into deep soundings, particularly delight and torture me. Something must have happened in such places, and perhaps ages back, to members of my race; and when I was a child I tried to invent appropriate games for them, as I still try, just as vainly, to fit them with the proper story. Some places speak distinctly. Certain dank gardens cry aloud for a murder; certain old houses demand to be haunted; certain coasts are set aside for shipwreck. Other spots again seem to abide their destiny, suggestive and impenetrable, "miching mallecho." The inn at Burford Bridge, with its arbours and green garden and silent, eddying river though it is known already as the place where Keats wrote some of his *Endymion* and Nelson parted from his Emma—still seems to wait the coming of the appropriate legend. Within these ivied walls, behind these old green shutters, some further business smoulders, waiting for its hour. The old Hawes Inn at the Queen's ferry makes a similar call upon my fancy. There it stands, apart from the town, beside the pier, in a climate of its own, half inland, half marine in front, the ferry bubbling with the tide and the guard-ship swinging to her anchor; behind, the old garden with the trees. Americans seek it already for the sake of Lovel and Oldbuck, who dined there at the beginning of the *Antiquary*. But you need not tell me, that is not all; there is some story, unrecorded or not yet complete, which must express the meaning of that inn more fully.... I have lived both at the Hawes and Burford in a perpetual flutter, on the heel, as it seemed, of some adventure that should justify the place; but though the feeling had me to bed at night and called me again at morning in one unbroken round of pleasure and suspense, nothing befell me in either worth remark. The man or the hour had not yet come; but some day, I think, a boat shall put off from the Queen's ferry, fraught with a dear cargo, and some frosty night a horseman, on a tragic errand, rattle with his whip upon the green shutters at the inn at Burford.

—**R.L. STEVENSON**, *A Gossip on Romance*

From "Midnight in London"

Clang! Clang! Clang! the fire-bells! Bing! Bing! Bing! the alarm! In an instant quiet turns to uproar—an outburst of noise, excitement, clamor—bedlam broke loose; Bing! Bing! Bing! Rattle, clash and clatter. Open fly the doors; brave men mount their boxes. Bing! Bing! Bing! They're off! The horses tear down the street like mad. Bing! Bing! Bing! goes the gong!

"Get out of the track! The engines are coming! For God's sake, snatch that child from the road!"

On, on, wildly, resolutely, madly fly the steeds. Bing! Bing! the gong. Away dash the horses on the wings of fevered fury. On whirls the machine, down streets, around corners, up this avenue and across that one, out into the very bowels of darkness, whiffing, wheezing, shooting a million sparks from the stack, paving the path of startled night with a galaxy of stars. Over the house-tops to the north, a volcanic burst of flame shoots out, belching with blinding effect. The sky is ablaze. A tenement house is burning. Five hundred souls are in peril. Merciful

Heaven! Spare the victims! Are the engines coming? Yes, here they are, dashing down the street. Look! the horses ride upon the wind; eyes bulging like balls of fire; nostrils wide open. A palpitating billow of fire, rolling, plunging, bounding rising, falling, swelling, heaving, and with mad passion bursting its red-hot sides asunder, reaching out its arms, encircling, squeezing, grabbing up, swallowing everything before it with the hot, greedy mouth of an appalling monster.

How the horses dash around the corner! Animal instinct say you? Aye, more. Brute reason.

"Up the ladders, men!"

The towering building is buried in bloated banks of savage, biting elements. Forked tongues dart out and in, dodge here and there, up and down, and wind their cutting edges around every object. A crash, a dull, explosive sound, and a puff of smoke leaps out. At the highest point upon the roof stands a dark figure in a desperate strait, the hands making frantic gestures, the arms swinging wildly—and then the body shoots off into frightful space, plunging upon the pavement with a revolting thud. The man's arm strikes a bystander as he darts down. The crowd shudders, sways, and utters a low murmur of pity and horror. The faint-hearted on lookers hide their faces. One woman swoons away.

"Poor fellow! Dead!" exclaims a labourer, as he looks upon the man's body.

"Aye, Joe, and I knew him well, too! He lived next door to me, five flights back. He leaves a widowed mother and two wee bits of orphans. I helped him bury his wife a fortnight ago. Ah, Joe! but it's hard lines for the orphans."

A ghastly hour moves on, dragging its regiment of panic in its trail and leaving crimson blotches of cruelty along the path of night.

"Are they all out, firemen?"

"Aye, aye, sir!"

"No, they're not! There's a woman in the top window

holding a child in her arms over yonder in the right-hand corner! The ladders, there! A hundred pounds to the man who makes the rescue!"

A dozen start. One man more supple than the others, and reckless in his bravery, clambers to the top rung of the ladder.

"Too short!" he cries. "Hoist another!"

Up it goes. He mounts to the window, fastens the rope, lashes mother and babe, swings them off into ugly emptiness, and lets them down to be rescued by his comrades.

"Bravo, fireman!" shouts the crowd.

A crash breaks through the uproar of crackling timbers.

"Look alive, up there! Great God! The roof has fallen!"

The walls sway, rock, and tumble in with a deafening roar. The spectators cease to breathe. The cold truth reveals itself. The fireman has been carried into the seething furnace. An old woman, bent with the weight of age, rushes through the fire line, shrieking, raving, and wringing her hands and opening her heart of grief.

"Poor John! He was all I had! And a brave lad he was, too! But he's gone now. He lost his own life in savin' two more, and now, now he's there, away in there!" she repeats, pointing to the cruel oven.

The engines do their work. The flames die out. An eerie gloom hangs over the ruins like a formidable, blackened pall.

And the noon of night is passed.

—**ARDENNES JONES-FOSTER**

□

21

Influencing by Narration

The art of narration is the art of writing in hooks and eyes. The principle consists in making the appropriate thought follow the appropriate thought, the proper fact the proper fact; in first preparing the mind for what is to come, and then letting it come.

—**WALTER BAGEHOT**, *Literary Studies*

Our very speech is curiously historical. Most men, you may observe, speak only to narrate; not in imparting what they have thought, which indeed were often a very small matter, but in exhibiting what they have undergone or seen, which is a quite unlimited one, do talkers dilate. Cut us off from Narrative, how would the stream of conversation, even among the wisest, languish into detached handfuls, and among the foolish utterly evaporate! Thus, as we do nothing but enact History, we say little but recite it.

—**THOMAS CARLYLE**, *On History*

Only a small segment of the great field of narration offers its resources to the public speaker, and that includes the anecdote, biographical facts, and the narration of events in general.

Narration, more easily defined than mastered, is the recital of an incident, or a group of facts and occurrences, in such a manner as to produce a desired effect.

The laws of narration are few, but its successful practice involves more of art than would at first appear, so much, indeed, that we cannot even touch upon its technique here, but must content ourselves with an examination of a few examples of narration as used in public speech.

In a preliminary way, notice how radically the public speaker's use of narrative differs from that of the story-writer in the more limited scope, absence of extended dialogue and character drawing, and freedom from elaboration of detail, which characterise platform narrative. On the other hand, there are several similarities of method: the frequent combination of narration with exposition, description, argumentation, and pleading; the care exercised in the arrangement of material so as to produce a strong effect at the close (climax); the very general practice of concealing the "point" (denouement) of a story until the effective moment; and the careful suppression of needless, and therefore hurtful, details.

So we see that, whether for magazine or platform, the art of narration involves far more than the recital of annals; the succession of events recorded requires a *plan* in order to bring them out with real effect.

It will be noticed, too, that the literary style in platform narration is likely to be either less polished and more vigorously dramatic than in that intended for publication, or else more fervid and elevated in tone. In this latter respect, however, the best platform speaking of today differs from the models of the preceding generation, wherein a highly dignified, and sometimes pompous, style was thought the only fitting dress for a public deliverance. Great, noble and stirring as these older masters were in their lofty and impassioned eloquence, we are sometimes oppressed when we read their sounding periods for any great length of time—even allowing for all that we lose by missing the speaker's presence, voice, and fire. So let us model our platform narration, as our other forms of speech, upon the effective addresses of the moderns, without lessening our admiration for the older school.

The Anecdote

An anecdote is a short narrative of a single event, told as being striking enough to bring out a point. The keener the point, the more condensed the form, and the more suddenly the application strikes the listener, the better the story.

To regard an anecdote as an illustration, an interpretive picture, will help to hold us to its true purpose, for a purposeless story is of all offences on the platform the most asinine. A perfectly capital joke will fall flat when it is dragged in by the nape without evident bearing on the subject under discussion. On the other hand, an apposite anecdote has saved many a speech from failure.

"There is no finer opportunity for the display of tact than in the introduction of witty or humorous stories into a discourse. Wit is keen and like a rapier, piercing deeply, sometimes even to the heart. Humour is good-natured, and does not wound. Wit is founded upon the sudden discovery of an unsuspected relation existing between two ideas. Humor deals with things out of relation—with the incongruous. It was wit in Douglass Jerrold to retort upon the scowl of a stranger whose shoulder he had familiarly slapped, mistaking him for a friend: 'I beg your pardon, I thought I knew you—but I'm glad I don't.' It was humour in the Southern orator, John Wise, to liken the pleasure of spending an evening with a Puritan girl to that of sitting on a block of ice in winter, cracking hailstones between his teeth."[J.Berg Esenwein]

The foregoing quotation has been introduced chiefly to illustrate the first and simplest form of anecdote—the single sentence embodying a pungent saying.

Another simple form is that which conveys its meaning without need of "application," as the old preachers used to say. George Ade has quoted this one as the best joke he ever heard:

'Two solemn-looking gentlemen were riding together in a railway carriage. One gentleman said to the other: "Is your wife entertaining this summer?" Whereupon the other gentleman replied: "Not very.'

Other anecdotes need harnessing to the particular truth the speaker wishes to carry along in his talk. Sometimes the application is made before the story is told and the audience is prepared to make the comparison, point by point, as the illustration is told. Henry W. Grady used this method in one of the anecdotes he told while delivering his great extemporaneous address, "The New South."

Age does not endow all things with strength and virtue, nor are all new things to be despised. The shoemaker who put over his door, "John Smith's shop, founded 1760," was more than matched by his young rival across the street who hung out this sign:

"Bill Jones. Established 1886. No old stock kept in this shop."

In two anecdotes, told also in "The New South," Mr. Grady illustrated another way of enforcing the application: in both instances he split the idea he wished to drive home, bringing in part before and part after the recital of the story. The fact that the speaker misquoted the words of Genesis in which the Ark is described did not seem to detract from the burlesque humour of the story.

'I bespeak the utmost stretch of your courtesy tonight. I am not troubled about those from whom I come. You remember the man whose wife sent him to a neighbour with a pitcher of milk, who, tripping on the top step, fell, with such casual interruptions as the landings afforded, into the basement, and, while picking himself up, had the pleasure of hearing his wife call out':

"John, did you break the pitcher"?

"No, I didn't," said John, "but I be dinged if I don't."

So, while those who call to me from behind may inspire me with energy, if not with courage, I ask an indulgent hearing from you. I beg that you will bring your full faith in American fairness and frankness to judgement upon what I shall say. There was an old preacher once who told some boys of the Bible lesson he was going to read in the morning. The boys, finding the place, glued together the connecting pages. The next morning he read on the bottom of one page: "When Noah was one hundred and twenty years old he took unto himself a wife, who was", then turning the page,"one hundred and forty cubits long, forty cubits wide, built of gopher wood, and covered with pitch inside and out." He was naturally puzzled at this. He read it again, verified it, and then said, "My friends, this is the first time I ever met this in the Bible, but I accept it as an evidence of the assertion that we are fearfully and wonderfully made." If I could get you to hold such faith tonight, I could proceed cheerfully to the task I otherwise approach with a sense of consecration.

Now and then a speaker will plunge without introduction into an anecdote, leaving the application to follow. The following illustrates this method:

"A large, slew-footed darky was leaning against the corner of the railroad station in a Texas town when the noon whistle in the canning factory blew and the hands hurried out, bearing their grub buckets. The darky listened, with his head on one side until the rocketing echo had quite died away. Then he heaved a deep sigh and remarked to himself":

"Dar she go. Dinner time for some folks, but jes' 12 o'clock fur me!"

"That is the situation in thousands of American factories, large and small, today. And why? etc., etc."

Doubtless the most frequent platform use of the anecdote is in the pulpit. The sermon "illustration," however, is not always strictly narrative in form, but tends to extended comparison, as the following from Dr. Alexander Maclaren:

"Men will stand as Indian fakirs do, with their arms above their heads until they stiffen there. They will perch themselves upon pillars like Simeon Stylites, for years, till the birds build their nests in their hair. They will measure all the distance from Cape Comorin to Juggernaut's temple with their bodies along the dusty road. They will wear hair shirts and scourge themselves. They will fast and deny themselves. They will build cathedrals and endow churches. They will do as many of you do, labour by fits and starts all through your lives at the endless task of making yourselves ready for heaven, and winning it by obedience and by righteousness. They will do all these things and do them gladly, rather than listen to the humbling message that says, "You do not need to do anything, wash." Is it your washing, or the water, that will clean you? Wash and be clean! Naaman's cleaning was only a test of his obedience, and a token that it was God who cleansed him. There was no power in Jordan's waters to take away the taint of leprosy. Our cleansing is in that blood of Jesus Christ that has the power to take away all sin, and to make the foulest amongst us pure and clean."

One final word must be said about the introduction to the anecdote. A clumsy, inappropriate introduction is fatal, whereas a single apt or witty sentence will kindle interest and prepare a favourable hearing. The following extreme illustration, by the English humorist, Captain Harry Graham, well satirises the stumbling manner:

"The best story that I ever heard was one that I was told once in the fall of 1905 (or it may have been 1906), when I was visiting Boston, at least, I think it was Boston; it may have been Washington (my memory is so bad).

I happened to run across a most amusing man whose name I forget, Williams or Wilson or Wilkins; some name like that, and he told me this story while we were waiting for a trolley car.

I can still remember how heartily I laughed at the time; and again, that evening, after I had gone to bed, how I laughed myself to sleep recalling the humour of this incredibly humorous story. It was really quite extraordinarily funny. In fact, I can truthfully affirm that it is quite the most amusing story I have ever had the privilege of hearing. Unfortunately, I've forgotten it."

Biographical Facts

Public speaking has much to do with personalities; naturally, therefore, the narration of a series of biographical details, including anecdotes among the recital of interesting facts, plays a large part in the eulogy, the memorial address, the political speech, the sermon, the lecture, and other platform deliverances. Whole addresses may be made up of such biographical details, such as a sermon on "Moses," or a lecture on "Lee."

Here is an example, prefaced by a general historical statement and concluding with autobiographical details:

A REMINISCENCE OF LEXINGTON

One raw morning in spring—it will be eighty years the 19th day of this month—Hancock and Adams, the Moses and Aaron of that Great Deliverance, were both at Lexington; they also had "obstructed an officer" with brave words. British soldiers, a thousand strong, came to seize them and carry them over sea for trial, and so nip the bud of Freedom auspiciously opening in that early spring. The town militia came together before daylight, "for training." A great, tall man, with a large head and a high, wide brow, their captain,—one who had "seen service,"—marshalled them into line, numbering but seventy, and bade "everyman load his piece with powder and ball. I will order the first man shot that runs away," said he, when some faltered. "Don't fire unless fired upon, but if they want to have a war, let it begin here."

Gentlemen, you know what followed; those farmers and mechanics "fired the shot heard round the world." A little monument covers the bones of such as before had pledged their fortune and their sacred honour to the Freedom of America, and that day gave it also their lives. I was born in that little town, and bred up amid the memories of that day. When a boy, my mother lifted me up, one Sunday, in her religious, patriotic arms, and held me while I read the first monumental line I ever saw, "Sacred to Liberty and the Rights of Mankind."

Since then I have studied the memorial marbles of Greece and Rome, in many an ancient town; nay, on Egyptian obelisks have read what was written before the Eternal raised up Moses to lead Israel out of Egypt; but no chiselled stone has ever stirred me to such emotion as these rustic names of men who fell "In the Sacred Cause of God and their Country."

Gentlemen, the Spirit of Liberty, the Love of Justice, were early fanned into a flame in my boyish heart. That monument covers the bones of my own kinsfolk; it was their blood which reddened the long, green grass at Lexington. It was my own name which stands chiselled on that stone; the tall captain who marshalled his fellow farmers and mechanics into stern array, and spoke such brave and dangerous words as opened the war of American Independence, the last to leave the field, was my father's father. I learned to read out of his Bible, and with a musket he that day captured from the foe, I learned another religious lesson, that "Rebellion to Tyrants is Obedience to God." I keep them both "Sacred to Liberty and the Rights of Mankind," to use them both "In the Sacred Cause of God and my Country."

—THEODORE PARKER

Narration of Events in General

In this wider, emancipated narration we find much mingling of other forms of discourse, greatly to the advantage of the speech, for this truth cannot be too strongly emphasized: The efficient speaker cuts loose from form for the sake of a big, free effect. The present analyses are for no other purpose than to *acquaint* you with form, do not allow any such models to hang as a weight about your neck.

The following pure narration of events, from George William Curtis's "Paul Revere's Ride," varies the biographical recital in other parts of his famous oration:

"That evening, at ten o'clock, eight hundred British troops, under Lieutenant-Colonel Smith, took boat at the foot of the Common and crossed to the Cambridge shore. Gage thought his secret had been kept, but Lord Percy, who had heard the people say on the Common that the troops would miss their aim, undeceived him. Gage instantly ordered that no one should leave the town. But as the troops crossed the river, Ebenezer Dorr, with a message to Hancock and Adams, was riding over the Neck to Roxbury, and Paul Revere was rowing over the river to Charlestown, having agreed with his friend, Robert Newman, to show lanterns from the belfry of the Old North Church, "One if by land, and two if by sea", as a signal of the march of the British."

The following, from the same oration, beautifully mingles description with narration:

"It was a brilliant night. The winter had been unusually mild, and the spring very forward. The hills were already green. The early grain waved in the fields, and the air was sweet with the blossoming orchards. Already the robins whistled, the bluebirds sang, and the benediction of peace rested upon the landscape. Under the cloudless moon the soldiers silently marched, and Paul Revere swiftly rode, galloping through Medford and West Cambridge, rousing every house as he went spurring for Lexington and Hancock and Adams, and evading the British patrols who had been sent out to stop the news."

In the succeeding extract from another of Mr. Curtis's addresses, we have a free use of allegory as illustration:

The Leadership of Educated Men

There is a modern English picture which the genius of Hawthorne might have inspired. The painter calls it, "How they met themselves." A man and a woman, haggard and weary, wandering lost in a sombre wood, suddenly meet the shadowy figures of a youth and a maid. Some mysterious fascination fixes the gaze and stills the hearts of the wanderers, and their amazement deepens into awe as they gradually recognize themselves as once they were; the soft bloom of youth upon their rounded cheeks, the dewy light of hope in their trusting eyes, exulting confidence in their springing step, themselves blithe and radiant with the glory of the dawn. Today, and here, we meet ourselves. Not to these familiar scenes alone, yonder college-green with its reverend traditions; the halcyon cove of the Seekonk, upon which the memory of Roger Williams broods like a bird of calm; the historic bay, beating forever with the muffled oars of Barton and of Abraham Whipple; here, the humming city of the living; there, the peaceful city of the dead; not to these only or chiefly do we return, but to ourselves as we once were. It is not the smiling freshmen of the year, it is your own beardless and unwrinkled faces, that are looking from the windows of University Hall and of Hope College. Under the trees upon the hill it is yourselves whom you see walking, full of hopes and dreams, glowing with conscious power, and "nourishing a youth sublime;" and in this familiar temple, which surely has never echoed with eloquence so fervid and inspiring as that of your commencement orations, it is not yonder youths in the galleries who, as they fondly believe, are whispering to yonder maids; it is your younger selves who, in the days that are no more, are murmuring to the fairest mothers and grandmothers of those maids.

Happy the worn and weary man and woman in the picture could they have felt their older eyes still glistening with that earlier light, and their hearts yet beating with undiminished sympathy and aspiration. Happy we, brethren, whatever may have been achieved, whatever left undone, if, returning to the home of our earlier years, we bring with us the illimitable hope, the unchilled resolution, the inextinguishable faith of youth.

—**GEORGE WILLIAM CURTIS**

□

22

Influencing by Suggestion

> Sometimes the feeling that a given way of looking at things is undoubtedly correct prevents the mind from thinking at all.... In view of the hindrances which certain kinds or degrees of feeling throw into the way of thinking, it might be inferred that the thinker must suppress the element of feeling in the inner life. No greater mistake could be made. If the Creator endowed man with the power to think, to feel, and to will, these several activities of the mind are not designed to be in conflict, and so long as any one of them is not perverted or allowed to run to excess, it necessarily aids and strengthens the others in their normal functions.
>
> —**NATHAN C. SCHAEFFER**
>
> *Thinking and Learning to Think*

When we weigh, compare, and decide upon the value of any given ideas, we reason; when an idea produces in us an opinion or an action, without first being subjected to deliberation, we are moved by suggestion.

Man was formerly thought to be a reasoning animal, basing his actions on the conclusions of natural logic. It was supposed that before forming an opinion or deciding on a course of conduct he weighed at least some of the reasons for and against the matter, and performed a more or less simple process of reasoning. But modern research has shown that quite the opposite is true. Most of our opinions and actions are not based upon conscious reasoning, but are the result of suggestion. In fact, some authorities declare that an act of pure reasoning is very rare in the average mind. Momentous decisions are made, far-reaching actions are determined upon, primarily by the force of suggestion.

Notice that word "primarily," for simple thought, and even mature reasoning, often follows a suggestion accepted in the mind, and the thinker fondly supposes that his conclusion is from first to last based on cold logic.

The Basis of Suggestion

We must think of suggestion both as an effect and as a cause. Considered as an effect, or objectively, there must be something in the listener that predisposes him to receive suggestion; considered as a cause, or subjectively, there must be some methods by which the speaker can move upon that particularly susceptible attitude of the listener. How to do this honestly and fairly is our problem—to do it dishonestly and trickily, to use suggestion to bring about conviction and action without a basis of right and truth and in a bad cause, is to assume the terrible responsibility that must fall on the champion of error. Jesus scorned not to use suggestion so that he might move men to their benefit, but every vicious trickster has adopted the same means to reach base ends. Therefore honest men will examine well into their motives and into the truth of their cause, before seeking to influence men by suggestion.

Three fundamental conditions make us all susceptive to suggestion:

We naturally respect authority. In every mind this is only a question of degree, ranging from the subject who is easily hypnotised to the stubborn mind that fortifies itself the more strongly with every assault upon its opinion. The latter type is almost immune to suggestion.

One of the singular things about suggestion is that it is rarely a fixed quantity. The mind that is receptive to the authority of a certain person may prove inflexible to another; moods and environments that produce hypnosis readily in one instance may be entirely inoperative in another; and some minds can scarcely ever be thus moved. We do know, however, that the feeling of the subject that authority, influence, power, domination, control, whatever you wish to call it, lies in the person of the suggester, is the basis of all suggestion.

The extreme force of this influence is demonstrated in hypnotism. The hypnotic subject is told that he is in the water; he accepts the statement as true and makes swimming motions. He is told that a band is marching down the street, playing "The Star Spangled Banner;" he declares he hears the music, arises and stands with head bared.

In the same way some speakers are able to achieve a modified hypnotic effect upon their audiences. The listeners will applaud measures and ideas which, after individual reflection, they will repudiate unless such reflection brings the conviction that the first impression is correct.

A second important principle is that *our feelings, thoughts and wills tend to follow the line of least resistance.* Once open the mind to the sway of one feeling and it requires a greater power of feeling, thought, or will, or even all three, to unseat it. Our feelings influence our judgements and volitions much more than we care to admit. So true is this that it is a superhuman task to get an audience to reason fairly on a subject on which it feels deeply, and when this result is accomplished the success becomes noteworthy, as in the case of Henry Ward Beecher's Liverpool speech. Emotional ideas once accepted are soon cherished, and finally become our very inmost selves. Attitudes based on feelings alone are prejudices.

What is true of our feelings, in this respect, applies to our ideas: All thoughts that enter the mind tend to be accepted as truth unless a stronger and contradictory thought arises.

The speaker skilled in moving men to action manages to dominate the minds of his audience with his thoughts by subtly prohibiting the entertaining of ideas hostile to his own. Most of us are captured by the latest strong attack, and if we can be induced to act while under the stress of that last insistent thought, we lose sight of counter influences. The fact is that almost all our decisions, if they involve thought at all are of this sort: At the moment of decision the course of action then under contemplation usurps the attention, and conflicting ideas are dropped out of consideration.

The head of a large publishing house remarked only recently that ninety per cent of the people who bought books by subscription never read them. They buy because the salesman presents his wares so skilfully that every consideration but the attractiveness of the book drops out of the mind, and that thought prompts action. *Every* idea that enters the mind will result in action unless a contradictory thought arises to prohibit it. Think of singing the musical scale and it will result in your singing it unless the counter-thought of its futility or absurdity inhibits your action. If you bandage and "doctor" a horse's foot, he will go lame. You cannot think of swallowing, without the muscles used in that process being affected. You cannot think of saying "hello," without a slight movement of the muscles of speech. To warn children that they should not put beans up their noses is the surest method of getting them to do it. Every thought called up in the mind of your audience will work either for or against you. Thoughts are not dead matter; they radiate dynamic energy, the thoughts all tend to pass into action. "Thought is another name for fate." Dominate your listeners' thoughts, allay all contradictory ideas, and you will sway them as you wish.

Volitions as well as feelings and thoughts tend to follow

the line of least resistance. That is what makes habit. Suggest to a man that it is impossible to change his mind and in most cases it becomes more difficult to do so, the exception is the man who naturally jumps to the contrary. Counter suggestion is the only way to reach him. Suggest subtly and persistently that the opinions of those in the audience who are opposed to your views are changing, and it requires an effort of the will—in fact, a summoning of the forces of feeling, thought and will—to stem the tide of change that has subconsciously set in.

But, not only are we moved by authority, and tend towards channels of least resistance: *We are all influenced by our environments.* It is difficult to rise above the sway of a crowd—its enthusiasms and its fears are contagious because they are suggestive. What so many feel, we say to ourselves, must have some basis in truth. Ten times ten makes more than one hundred. Set ten men to speaking to ten audiences of ten men each, and compare the aggregate power of those ten speakers with that of one man addressing one hundred men. The ten speakers may be more logically convincing than the single orator, but the chances are strongly in favour of the one man's reaching a greater total effect, for the hundred men will radiate conviction and resolution as ten small groups could not. We all know the truism about the enthusiasm of numbers. (See the chapter on "Influencing the Crowd.")

Environment controls us unless the contrary is strongly suggested. A gloomy day, in a drab room, sparsely tenanted by listeners, invites platform disaster. Everyone feels it in the air. But let the speaker walk squarely up to the issue and suggest by all his feeling, manner and words that this is going to be a great gathering in every vital sense, and see how the suggestive power of environment recedes before the advance of a more potent suggestion—if such the speaker is able to make it.

Now these three factors, respect for authority, tendency to follow lines of least resistance, and susceptibility to environment all help to bring the audience into a state of mind favourable to suggestive influences, but they also react on the speaker, and now we must consider those personally causative, or subjective, forces which enable him to use suggestion effectively.

How the Speaker Can Make Suggestion Effective

We have seen that under the influence of authoritative suggestion the audience is inclined to accept the speaker's assertion without argument and criticism. But the audience is not in this state of mind unless it has implicit confidence in the speaker. If they lack faith in him, question his motives or knowledge, or even object to his manner they will not be moved by his most logical conclusion and will fail to give him a just hearing. *It is all a matter of their confidence in him.* Whether the speaker finds it already in the warm, expectant look of his listeners, or must win to it against opposition or coldness, he must gain that one great vantage point before his suggestions take on power in the hearts of his listeners. Confidence is the mother of Conviction.

Note in the opening of Henry W. Grady's after-dinner speech how he attempted to secure the confidence of his audience. He created a receptive atmosphere by a humorous story; expressed his desire to speak with earnestness and sincerity; acknowledged "the vast interests involved;" deprecated his "untried arm," and professed his humility. Would not such an introduction give you confidence in the speaker, unless you were strongly opposed to him? And even then, would it not partly disarm your antagonism?

Mr. President: Bidden by your invitation to a discussion of the race problem forbidden by occasion to make a political speech I appreciate, in trying to reconcile orders with propriety, the perplexity of the little maid, who, bidden to learn to swim, was yet adjured, "Now, go, my darling; hang your clothes on a hickory limb, and don't go near the water."

The stoutest apostle of the Church, they say, is the

missionary, and the missionary, wherever he unfurls his flag, will never find himself in deeper need of unction and address than I, bidden tonight to plant the standard of a Southern Democrat in Boston's banquet hall, and to discuss the problem of the races in the home of Phillips and of Sumner. But, Mr. President, if a purpose to speak in perfect frankness and sincerity; if earnest understanding of the vast interests involved; if a consecrating sense of what disaster may follow further misunderstanding and estrangement; if these may be counted to steady undisciplined speech and to strengthen an untried arm then, sir, I shall find the courage to proceed.

Note also Bryan's attempt to secure the confidence of his audience in the following introduction to his "Cross of Gold" speech delivered before the National Democratic Convention in Chicago, 1896. He asserts his own inability to oppose the "distinguished gentleman;" he maintains the holiness of his cause; and he declares that he will speak in the interest of humanity—well knowing that humanity is likely to have confidence in the champion of their rights. This introduction completely dominated the audience, and the speech made Bryan famous.

"Mr. Chairman and Gentlemen of the Convention: I would be presumptuous indeed to present myself against the distinguished gentlemen to whom you have listened if this were a mere measuring of abilities; but this is not a contest between persons. The humblest citizen in all the land, when clad in the armour of a righteous cause, is stronger than all the hosts of error. I come to speak to you in defence of a cause as holy as the cause of liberty, the cause of humanity."

Some speakers are able to beget confidence by their very manner, while others cannot.

To secure confidence, be confident. How can you expect others to accept a message in which you lack, or seem to lack, faith yourself? Confidence is as contagious as disease. Napoleon rebuked an officer for using the word "impossible" in his presence. The speaker who will entertain no idea of defeat begets in his listeners the idea of his victory. Lady Macbeth was so confident of success that Macbeth changed his mind about undertaking the assassination. Columbus was so certain in his mission that Queen Isabella pawned her jewels to finance his expedition. Assert your message with implicit assurance, and your own belief will act as so much gunpowder to drive it home.

Advertisers have long utilised this principle. "The machine you will eventually buy," "Ask the man who owns one," "Has the strength of Gibraltar," are publicity slogans so full of confidence that they give birth to confidence in the mind of the reader.

It should but may not! go without saying that confidence must have a solid ground of merit or there will be a ridiculous crash. It is all very well for the "spellbinder" to claim all the precinctsthe official count is just ahead. The reaction against over-confidence and over-suggestion ought to warn those whose chief asset is mere bluff.

A short time ago a speaker arose in a public-speaking club and asserted that grass would spring from wood-ashes sprinkled over the soil, without the aid of seed. This idea was greeted with a laugh, but the speaker was so sure of his position that he reiterated the statement forcefully several times and cited his own personal experience as proof. One of the most intelligent men in the audience, who at first had derided the idea, at length came to believe in it. When asked the reason for his sudden change of attitude, he replied: "Because the speaker is so confident."

If by a speaker's confidence, intelligent men can be made to believe such preposterous theories as this where will the power of self-reliance cease when plausible propositions are under consideration, advanced with all the power of convincing speech?

Note the utter assurance in these selections:

I know not what course others may take, but as for me give me liberty or give me death.

—PATRICK HENRY

I ne'er will ask ye quarter, and I ne'er will be your slave;
But I'll swim the sea of slaughter, till I sink beneath its wave.

—PATTEN

Come one, come all. This rock shall fly From its firm base as soon as I.

—SIR WALTER SCOTT

Authority is a factor in suggestion. We generally accept as truth, and without criticism, the words of an authority. When he speaks, contradictory ideas rarely arise in the mind to inhibit the action he suggests. A judge of the Supreme Court has the power of his words multiplied by the virtue of his position.

This principle also has been used in advertising. We are told that the physicians to two Kings have recommended a particulars Sanatogen. We are informed that the largest bank in America, Tiffany and Co., and The State, War, and Navy Departments, all use the Encyclopaedia Britannica. The shrewd promoter gives stock in his company to influential bankers or business men in the community in order that he may use their examples as a selling argument.

If you wish to influence your audience through suggestion, if you would have your statements accepted without criticism or argument, you should appear in the light of an authority and *be* one. Ignorance and credulity will remain unchanged unless the suggestion of authority be followed promptly by facts. Don't claim authority unless you carry your license in your pocket. Let reason support the position that suggestion has assumed.

Advertising will help to establish your reputation it is "up to you" to maintain it. One speaker found that his reputation as a magazine writer was a splendid asset as a speaker. But, back of it all, Newspaper announcements, all kinds of advertising, formality, impressive introductions, all have a capital effect on the attitude of the audience. But how ridiculous are all these if a toy pistol is advertised as a sixteen-inch gun!

Note how authority is used in the following to support the strength of the speaker's appeal:

"Professor Alfred Russell Wallace has just celebrated his 90th birthday. Sharing with Charles Darwin the honour of discovering evolution, Professor Wallace has lately received many and signal honours from scientific societies. At the dinner given him in London his address was largely made up of reminiscences. He reviewed the progress of civilisation during the last century and made a series of brilliant and startling contrasts between the England of 1813 and the world of 1913. He affirmed that our progress is only seeming and not real. Professor Wallace insists that the painters, the sculptors, the architects of Athens and Rome were so superior to the modern men that the very fragments of their marbles and temples are the despair of the presentday artists. He tells us that man has improved his telescope and spectacles, but that he is losing his eyesight; that man is improving his looms, but stiffening his fingers; improving his automobile and his locomotive, but losing his legs; improving his foods, but losing his digestion. He adds that the modern white slave traffic, orphan asylums, and tenement house life in factory towns, make a black page in the history of the twentieth century.

Professor Wallace's views are reinforced by the report of the commission of Parliament on the causes of the deterioration of the factory-class people. In our own country Professor Jordan warns us against war, intemperance, overworking, underfeeding of poor children, and disturbs our contentment with his "Harvest of Blood." Professor Jenks is more pessimistic. He thinks that the pace, the climate, and the stress of city life, have broken down the Puritan stock, that in another century our old families will be extinct, and that the flood of immigration means a Niagara of muddy waters fouling the pure springs of American life. In his address in New Haven Professor Kellogg calls the roll of the signs of race degeneracy and tells us that this deterioration even indicates a trend towards race extinction."

—**NEWELL DWIGHT HILLIS**

Authority is the great weapon against doubt, but even its force can rarely prevail against prejudice and persistent wrong headedness. If any speaker has been able to forge a sword that is warranted to piece such armour, let him bless humanity by sharing his secret with his platform brethren everywhere, for thus far he is alone in his glory.

There is a middle-ground between the suggestion of authority and the confession of weakness that offers a wide range for tact in the speaker. No one can advise you when to throw your "hat in the ring" and say defiantly at the outstart, "Gentlemen, I am here to fight!" It is for your own tact to decide whether you will use the disarming grace of Henry W. Grady's introduction just quoted (even the time-worn joke was ingenuous and seemed to say, "Gentlemen, I come to you with no carefully-palmed coins"), or whether the solemn gravity of Bryan will prove to be more effective. Only be sure that your opening attitude is well thoughtout, and if it changes as you warm up to your subject, let not the changes lay you open to a revulsion of feeling in your audience.

Example is a powerful means of suggestion. As we saw while thinking of environment in its effects on an audience, we do, without the usual amount of hesitation and criticism, what others are doing. Paris wears certain hats and gowns; the rest of the world imitates. The child mimics the actions, accents and intonations of the parent. Were a child never to hear anyone speak, he would never acquire the power of speech, unless under most arduous training, and even then only imperfectly. One of the biggest department stores in the United States spends fortunes on one advertising slogan: "Everybody is going to the big store." That makes everybody want to go.

You can reinforce the power of your message by showing that it has been widely accepted. Political organisations subsidise applause to create the impression that their speakers' ideas are warmly received and approved by the audience. The advocates of the commission-form of government of cities, the champions of votes for women, reserve as their strongest arguments the fact that a number of cities and states have already successfully accepted their plans. Advertisements use the testimonial for its power of suggestion.

Observe how this principle has been applied in the following selections, and utilise it on every occasion possible in your attempts to influence through suggestion:

"The war is actually begun. The next gale that sweeps from the North will bring to our ears the clash of resounding arms. Our brethren are already in the field. Why stand ye here idle?"

—PATRICK HENRY

Figurative and indirect language has suggestive force, because it does not make statements that can be directly disputed. It arouses no contradictory ideas in the minds of the audience, thereby fulfilling one of the basic requisites of suggestion. By *implying* a conclusion in indirect or figurative language it is often asserted most forcefully.

Note that in the following William Jeanings Bryan did not say that Mr. McKinley would be defeated. He implied it in a much more effective manner:

Mr. McKinley was nominated at St. Louis upon a platform which declared for the maintenance of the gold standard until it can be changed into bimetallism by international agreement. Mr. McKinley was the most popular man among the Republicans, and three months ago everybody in the Republican party prophesied his election. How is it today? Why, the man who was once pleased to think that he looked like Napoleon, that man shudders today when he remembers that he was nominated on the anniversary of the battle of Waterloo. Not only that, but as he listens he can hear with ever-increasing distinctness the sound of the waves as they beat upon the lonely shores of St. Helena.

Had Thomas Carlyle said: "A false man cannot found a religion," his words would have been neither so suggestive nor so powerful, nor so long remembered as his implication in these striking words:

A false man found a religion? Why, a false man cannot build a brick house! If he does not know and follow truly the properties of mortar, burnt clay, and what else he works in, it is no house that he makes, but a rubbish heap. It will not stand for twelve centuries, to lodge a hundred and eighty millions; it will fall straightaway. A man must conform himself to Nature's laws, be verily in communion with Nature and the truth of things, or Nature will answer him, No, not at all!

Observe how the picture that Webster draws here is much more emphatic and forceful than any mere assertion could be:

Sir, I know not how others may feel, but as for myself when I see my *alma mater* surrounded, like Caesar in the senate house, by those who are reiterating stab after stab, I would not for this right hand have her turn to me and say, "And thou, too, my son!"

—WEBSTER

A speech should be built on sound logical foundations, and no man should dare to speak in behalf of a fallacy. Arguing a subject, however, will necessarily arouse contradictory ideas in the mind of your audience. When immediate action or persuasion is desired, suggestion is more efficacious than argument—when both are judiciously mixed, the effect is irresistible.

□

3

Influencing by Argument

> Common sense is the common sense of mankind. It is the product of common observation and experience. It is modest, plain, and unsophisticated. It sees with everybody's eyes, and hears with everybody's ears. It has no capricious distinctions, no perplexities, and no mysteries. It never equivocates, and never trifles. Its language is always intelligible. It is known by clearness of speech and singleness of purpose.
>
> —**GEORGE JACOB HOLYOAKE**
>
> *Public Speaking and Debate*

The very name of logic is awesome to most young speakers, but so soon as they come to realize that its processes, even when most intricate, are merely technical statements of the truths enforced by common sense, it will lose its terrors. In fact, logic is a fascinating subject, well worth the public speaker's study, for it explains the principles that govern the use of argument and proof.

Argumentation is the process of producing conviction by means of reasoning. Other ways of producing conviction there are, notably suggestion, as we have just shown, but no means is so high, so worthy of respect, as the adducing of sound reasons in support of a contention.

Since more than one side of a subject must be considered before we can claim to have deliberated upon it fairly, we ought to think of argumentation under two aspects: building up an argument, and tearing down an argument; that is, you must not only examine into the stability of your structure of argument so that it may both support the proposition you intend to probe and yet be so sound that it cannot be overthrown by opponents, but you must also be so keen to detect defects in argument that you will be able to demolish the weaker arguments of those who argue against you.

The following series of questions will, it is hoped, serve a triple purpose: that of suggesting the forms of proof together with the ways in which they may be used; that of helping the speaker to test the strength of his arguments; and that of enabling the speaker to attack his opponent's arguments with both keenness and justice.

TESTING AN ARGUMENT

I. The Question Under Discussion

1. *Is it clearly stated?*
   (a) Do the terms of statement mean the same to each disputant? (For example, the meaning of the term "gentleman" may not be mutually agreed upon.)
   (b) Is confusion likely to arise as to its purpose?
2. *Is it fairly stated?*
   (a) Does it include enough?
   (b) Does it include too much?
   (c) Is it stated so as to contain a trap?
3. *Is it a debatable question?*
4. *What is the pivotal point in the whole question?*
5. What are the subordinate points?

II. The Evidence

1. *The witnesses as to facts*

(a) Is each witness impartial? What is his relation to the subject at issue?

(b) Is he mentally competent?

(c) Is he morally credible?

(d) Is he in a position to know the facts? Is he an eye-witness?

(e) Is he a willing witness?

(f) Is his testimony contradicted?

(g) Is his testimony corroborated?

(h) Is his testimony contrary to well-known facts or general principles?

(i) Is it probable?

2. *The authorities cited as evidence*

(a) Is the authority well-recognized as such?

(b) What constitutes him an authority?

(c) Is his interest in the case an impartial one?

(d) Does he state his opinion positively and clearly?

(e) Are the non-personal authorities cited (books, etc.) reliable and unprejudiced?

3. *The facts adduced as evidence*

(a) Are they sufficient in number to constitute proof?

(b) Are they weighty enough in character?

(c) Are they in harmony with reason?

(d) Are they mutually harmonious or contradictory?

(e) Are they admitted, doubted, or disputed?

4. *The principles adduced as evidence*

(a) Are they axiomatic?

(b) Are they truths of general experience?

(c) Are they truths of special experience?

(d) Are they truths arrived at by experiment?

Were such experiments special or general?

Were the experiments authoritative and conclusive?

III. The Reasoning

1. Inductions

(a) Are the facts numerous enough to warrant accepting the generalisation as being conclusive?

(b) Do the facts agree *only* when considered in the light of this explanation as a conclusion?

(c) Have you overlooked any contradictory facts?

(d) Are the contradictory facts sufficiently explained when this inference is accepted as true?

(e) Are all contrary positions shown to be relatively untenable?

(f) Have you accepted mere opinions as facts?

2. *Deductions*

(a) Is the law or general principle a well-established one?

(b) Does the law or principle clearly include the fact you wish to deduce from it, or have you strained the inference?

(c) Does the importance of the law or principle warrant so important an inference?

(d) Can the deduction be shown to prove too much?

3. *Parallel cases*

(a) Are the cases parallel at enough points to warrant an inference of similar cause or effect?

(b) Are the cases parallel at the vital point at issue?

(c) Has the parallelism been strained?

(d) Are there no other parallels that would point to a stronger contrary conclusion?

4. *Inferences*

(a) Are the antecedent conditions such as would make the allegation probable? (Character and opportunities of the accused, for example.)

(b) Are the signs that point to the inference either clear or numerous enough to warrant its acceptance as fact?

(c) Are the signs cumulative, and agreeable one with the other?

(d) Could the signs be made to point to a contrary conclusion?

5. *Syllogisms*

(a) Have any steps been omitted in the syllogisms? (Such as in a syllogism *in enthymeme*.) If so, test any such by filling out the syllogisms.

(b) Have you been guilty of stating a conclusion that really does not follow? (A *non-sequitur*.)

(c) Can your syllogism be reduced to an absurdity? (Reductio ad absurdum.)

□

24

Influencing by Persuasion

She hath prosperous art When she will play with reason and discourse, And well she can persuade.

—**SHAKESPEARE**, *Measure for Measure*

Him we call an artist who shall play on an assembly of men as a master on the keys of a piano, who seeing the people furious, shall soften and compose them, shall draw them, when he will, to laughter and to tears. Bring him to his audience, and, be they who they may, coarse or refined, pleased or displeased, sulky or savage, with their opinions in the keeping of a confessor or with their opinions in their bank safes, he will have them pleased and humoured as he chooses; and they shall carry and execute what he bids them.

—**RALPH WALDO EMERSON**
Essay on *Eloquence*

More good and more ill have been effected by persuasion than by any other form of speech. *It is an attempt to influence by means of appeal to some particular interest held important by the listeners.* Its motive may be high or low, fair or unfair, honest or dishonest, calm or passionate, and hence its scope is unparalleled in public speaking.

This "instilment of conviction," to use Matthew Arnold's expression, is naturally a complex process in that it usually includes argumentation and often employs suggestion, as the next chapter will illustrate. In fact, there is little public speaking worthy of the name that is not in some part persuasive, for men rarely speak solely to alter men's opinions the ulterior purpose is almost always action.

The nature of persuasion is not solely intellectual, but is largely emotional. It uses every principle of public speaking, and every "form of discourse," to use a rhetorician's expression, but argument supplemented by special appeal is its peculiar quality. This we may best see by examining the following:

The appeal to prejudice is effective, though not often, if ever, justifiable; yet so long as special pleading endures this sort of persuasion will be resorted to. Rudyard Kipling uses this method, as have many others on both sides, in discussing the great European war. Mingled with the appeal to prejudice, Mr. Kipling uses the appeal to self-interest; though not the highest, it is a powerful motive in all our lives. Notice how at the last the pleader sweeps on to the highest ground he can take. This is a notable example of progressive appeal, beginning with a low motive and ending with a high one in such a way as to carry all the force of prejudice yet gain all the value of patriotic fervour.

"Through no fault nor wish of ours we are at war with Germany, the power which owes its existence to three well-thought-out wars; the power which, for the last twenty years, has devoted itself to organising and preparing for this war; the power which is now fighting to conquer the civilised world.

For the last two generations the Germans in their books, lectures, speeches and schools have been carefully taught that nothing less than this world-conquest was the object of their preparations and their sacrifices. They have prepared carefully and sacrificed greatly.

We must have men and men and men, if we, with our allies, are to check the onrush of organized barbarism.

Have no illusions. We are dealing with a strong and magnificently equipped enemy, whose avowed aim is our complete destruction. The violation of Belgium, the attack on France and the defence against Russia, are only steps by the way. The German's real objective, as she always has told us, is England, and England's wealth, trade and worldwide possessions.

If you assume, for an instant, that the attack will be successful, England will not be reduced, as some people say, to the rank of a second rate power, but we shall cease to exist as a nation. We shall become an outlying province of Germany, to be administered with that severity German safety and interest require.

We are against such a fate. We enter into a new life in which all the facts of war that we had put behind or forgotten for the last hundred years, have returned to the front and test us as they tested our fathers. It will be a long and a hard road, beset with difficulties and discouragements, but we tread it together and we will tread it together to the end.

Our petty social divisions and barriers have been swept away at the outset of our mighty struggle. All the interests of our life of six weeks ago are dead. We have but one interest now, and that touches the naked heart of every man in this island and in the empire."

If we are to win the right for ourselves and for freedom to exist on earth, every man must offer himself for that service and that sacrifice."

From this example it will be seen that the particular way in which the audience: appealed to their listeners was *by coming close home to their interests, and by themselves showing emotion,* two very important principles which you must keep constantly in mind.

To accomplish the former requires a deep knowledge of human motive in general and an understanding of the particular audience addressed. What are the motives that arouse men to action? Think of them earnestly, set them down on the tablets of your mind, study how to appeal to them worthily. Then, what motives would be likely to appeal to *your* listeners? What are their ideals and interests in life? A mistake in your estimate may cost you your case. To appeal to pride in appearance would make one set of men merely laugh—to try to arouse sympathy for the Jews in Palestine would be wasted effort among others. Study your audience, feel your way, and when you have once raised a spark, fan it into a flame by every honest resource you possess.

The larger your audience the more sure you are to find a universal basis of appeal. A small audience of bachelors will not grow excited over the importance of furniture insurance; most men can be roused to the defence of the freedom of the press.

Patent medicine advertisement usually begins by talking about your pains they begin on your interests. If they first discussed the size and rating of their establishment, or the efficacy of their remedy, you would never read the "ad." If they can make you think you have nervous troubles you will even plead for a remedy—they will not have to try to sell it.

The patent medicine men are pleading asking you to invest your money in their commodity yet they do not appear to be doing so. They get over on your side of the fence, and arouse a desire for their nostrums by appealing to your own interests.

Recently a book-salesman entered an attorney's office in New York and inquired: "Do you want to buy a book?" Had the lawyer wanted a book he would probably have bought one without waiting for a book-salesman to call. The solicitor made the same mistake as the representative who made his approach with: "I want to sell you a sewing machine." They both talked only in terms of their own interests.

The successful pleader must convert his arguments into terms of his listeners' advantage. Mankind are still selfish, are interested in what will serve them. Expunge from your address your own personal concern and present your appeal in terms of the general good, and to do this you need not be insincere, for you had better not plead any cause that is *not* for the hearers' good. *Notice how Senator Thurston in his plea for intervention in Cuba and Mr. Bryan in his "Cross of Gold" speech constituted themselves the apostles of humanity.*

Exhortation is a highly impassioned form of appeal frequently used by the pulpit in efforts to arouse men to a sense of duty and induce them to decide their personal courses, and by counsel in seeking to influence a jury. The great preachers, like the great jury-lawyers, have always been masters of persuasion.

Notice the difference among these four exhortations, and analyse the motives appealed to:

"Revenge! About! Seek! Burn! Fire! Kill! Slay! Let not a traitor live!"

—**SHAKESPEARE,** *Julius Caesar*

"Strike till the last armed foe expires,
Strike for your altars and your fires,
Strike for the green graves of your sires,
God—and your native land!"

—**FITZ-GREENE HALLECK,** *Marco Bozzaris*

"Believe, gentlemen, if it were not for those children, he would not come here today to seek such remuneration; if it were not that, by your verdict, you may prevent those little innocent defrauded wretches from becoming wandering beggars, as well as orphans on the face of this earth. Oh, I know I need not ask this verdict from your mercy; I need not extort it from your compassion; I will receive it from your justice. I do conjure you, not as fathers, but as husbands:not as husbands, but as citizens: not as citizens, but as men: not as men, but as Christians: by all your obligations, public, private, moral, and religious; by the hearth profaned; by the home desolated; by the canons of the living God foully spurned; save, oh: save your firesides from the contagion, your country from the crime, and perhaps thousands, yet unborn, from the shame, and sin, and sorrow of this example!"

—CHARLES PHILLIPS

Appeal to the jury in behalf of Guthrie

"So I appeal from the men in silken hose who danced to music made by slaves and called it freedom, from the men in bell-crown hats who led Hester Prynne to her shame and called it religion, to that Americanism which reaches forth its arms to smite wrong with reason and truth, secure in the power of both. I appeal from the patriarchs of New England to the poets of New England; from Endicott to Lowell; from Winthrop to Longfellow; from Norton to Holmes; and I appeal in the name and by the rights of that common citizenship—of that common origin, back of both the Puritan and the Cavalier, to which all of us owe our being. Let the dead past, consecrated by the blood of its martyrs, not by its savage hatreds, darkened alike by kingcraft and priestcraft let the dead past bury its dead. Let the present and the future ring with the song of the singers. Blessed be the lessons they teach, the laws they make. Blessed be the eye to see, the light to reveal. Blessed be tolerance, sitting ever on the right hand of God to guide the way with loving word, as blessed be all that brings us nearer the goal of true religion, true republicanism, and true patriotism, distrust of watchwords and labels, shams and heroes, belief in our country and ourselves. It was not Cotton Mather, but John Greenleaf Whittier, who cried:

Dear God and Father of us all,
Forgive our faith in cruel lies,
Forgive the blindness that denies.
Cast down our idols—overturn
Our Bloody altars—make us see
Thyself in Thy humanity!"

—**HENRY WATTERSON**, *Puritan and Cavalier*

Goethe, on being reproached for not having written war songs against the French, replied, "In my poetry I have never shammed. How could I have written songs of hate without hatred?" Neither is it possible to plead with full efficiency for a cause for which you do not feel deeply. Feeling is contagious as belief is contagious. The speaker who pleads with real feeling for his own convictions will instil his feelings into his listeners. Sincerity, force, enthusiasm, and above all, feeling these are the qualities that move multitudes and make appeals irresistible. They are of far greater importance than technical principles of delivery, grace of gesture, or polished enunciation, important as all these elements must doubtless be considered. *Base* your appeal on reason, but do not end in the basement, let the building rise, full of deep emotion and noble persuasion.

□

25

Influencing the Crowd

> Success in business, in the last analysis, turns upon touching the imagination of crowds. The reason that preachers in this present generation are less successful in getting people to want goodness than business men are in getting them to want motorcars, hats, and pianolas, is that business men as a class are more close and desperate students of human nature, and have boned down harder to the art of touching the imaginations of the crowds.
>
> —**GERALD STANLEY LEE**, *Crowds*

In the early part of July, 1914, a collection of Frenchmen in Paris, or Germans in Berlin, was not a crowd in a psychological sense. Each individual had his own special interests and needs, and there was no powerful common idea to unify them. A group then represented only a collection of individuals. A month later, any collection of Frenchmen or Germans formed a crowd: Patriotism, hate, a common fear, a pervasive grief, had unified the individuals.

The psychology of the crowd is far different from the psychology of the personal members that compose it. The crowd is a distinct entity. Individuals restrain and subdue many of their impulses at the dictates of reason. The crowd never reasons. It only feels. As persons there is a sense of responsibility attached to our actions which checks many of our incitements, but the sense of responsibility is lost in the crowd because of its numbers. The crowd is exceedingly suggestible and will act upon the wildest and most extreme ideas. The crowd-mind is primitive and will cheer plans and perform actions which its members would utterly repudiate.

A mob is only a highly-wrought crowd. Ruskin's description is fitting: "You can talk a mob into anything; its feelings may be, usually are, on the whole, generous and right, but it has no foundation for them, no hold of them. You may tease or tickle it into anything at your pleasure. It thinks by infection, for the most part, catching an opinion like a cold, and there is nothing so little that it will not roar itself wild about, when the fit is on, nothing so great but it will forget in an hour when the fit is past."

History will show us how the crowd-mind works. The medieval mind was not given to reasoning; the medieval man attached great weight to the utterance of authority; his religion touched chiefly the emotions. These conditions provided a rich soil for the propagation of the crowd-mind when, in the eleventh century, flagellation, a voluntary self-scourging, was preached by the monks. Substituting flagellation for reciting penitential psalms was advocated by the reformers. A scale was drawn up, making one thousand strokes equivalent to ten psalms, or fifteen thousand to the entire psalter. This craze spread by leaps and crowds. Flagellant fraternities sprang up. Priests carrying banners led through the streets great processions reciting prayers and whipping their bloody bodies with leathern thongs fitted with four iron points. Pope Clement denounced this practice and several of the leaders of these processions had to be burned at the stake before the frenzy could be uprooted.

All western and central Europe was turned into a crowd by the preaching of the crusaders, and millions of the followers of the Prince of Peace rushed to the Holy Land to kill the heathen. Even the children started on a crusade against the Saracens. The mob-spirit was so strong that home affections and persuasion could not prevail against it and thousands of mere babes died in their attempts to reach and redeem the Sacred Sepulchre.

In the early part of the eighteenth century the South Sea Company was formed in England. Britain became a speculative crowd. Stock in the South Sea Company rose from 128-1/2 points in January to 550 in May, and scored 1,000 in July. Five million shares were sold at this premium. Speculation ran riot. Hundreds of companies were organised. One was formed "for a wheel of perpetual motion." Another never troubled to give any reason at all for taking the cash of its subscribers it merely announced that it was organised "for a design which will hereafter be promulgated." Owners began to sell, the mob caught the suggestion, a panic ensued, the South Sea Company stock fell 800 points in a few days, and more than a billion dollars evaporated in this era of frenzied speculation.

The burning of the witches at Salem, the Klondike gold craze, and the forty-eight people who were killed by mobs in the United States in 1913, are familiar examples to us in America.

The Crowd Must Have a Leader

The leader of the crowd or mob is its determining factor. He becomes self-hynoptised with the idea that unifies its members, his enthusiasm is contagious and so is theirs. The crowd acts as he suggests. The great mass of people do not have any very sharply-drawn conclusions on any subject outside of their own little spheres, but when they become a crowd they are perfectly willing to accept ready-made, hand-me-down opinions. They will follow a leader at all costs in labour troubles they often follow a leader in preference to obeying their government, in war they will throw self-preservation to the bushes and follow a leader in the face of guns that fire fourteen times a second. The mob becomes shorn of will-power and blindly obedient to its dictator. The Russian Government, recognising the menace of the crowd-mind to its autocracy, formerly prohibited public gatherings. History is full of similar instances.

How the Crowd is Created

Today the crowd is as real a factor in our socialised life as are magnates and monopolies. It is too complex a problem merely to damn or praise it—it must be reckoned with, and mastered. The present problem is how to get the most and the best out of the crowd-spirit, and the public speaker finds this to be peculiarly his own question. His influence is multiplied if he can only transmute his audience into a crowd. His affirmations must be their conclusions.

This can be accomplished by unifying the minds and needs of the audience and arousing their emotions. Their feelings, not their reason, must be played upon *it is "up to" him to do this nobly*. Argument has its place on the platform, but even its potencies must subserve the speaker's plan of attack to *win possession* of his audience.

Reread the chapter on "Feeling and Enthusiasm." It is impossible to make an audience a crowd without appealing to their emotions. Can you imagine the average group becoming a crowd while hearing a lecture on Dry Fly Fishing, or on Egyptian Art? On the other hand, it would not have required world-famous eloquence to have turned any audience in Ulster, in 1914, into a crowd by discussing the Home Rule Act. The crowd-spirit depends largely on the subject used to fuse their individualities into one glowing whole.

Ant. Now let it work. Mischief, thou art afoot,
Take thou what course thou wilt!

To unify single, listeners into a crowd, express their common needs, aspirations, dangers, and emotions, deliver your message so that the interests of one shall appear to be the interests of all. The conviction of one man is intensified in proportion as he finds others sharing his belief *and feeling*. Antony does not stop with telling the Roman populace that Caesar fell, he makes the tragedy universal:

"Then I, and you, and all of us fell down,
Whilst bloody treason flourished over us."

Applause, generally a sign of feeling, helps to unify an audience. The nature of the crowd is illustrated by the contagion of applause. A throng in a theatre had been applauding several songs, and when an advertisement for tailored skirts was thrown on the screen someone started the applause, and the crowd, like sheep, blindly imitated, until someone saw the joke and laughed; then the crowd again followed a leader and laughed at and applauded its own stupidity.

Actors sometimes start applause for their lines by snapping their fingers. Someone in the first few rows will mistake it for faint applause, and the whole theatre will chime in.

An observant audience will be interested in noticing the various devices a monologist will use to get the first round of laughter and applause. He works so hard because he knows an audience of units is an audience of indifferent critics, but once get them to laughing together and each single laugher sweeps a number of others with him, until the whole theatre is aroar and the entertainer has scored. Many a time has the popular preacher stopped in the middle of his talk, when he felt that his hearers were units instead of a molten mass (and a sensitive speaker can feel that condition most depressingly) and suddenly demanded that everyone arise and sing, or repeat aloud a familiar passage, or read in unison; or perhaps he has subtly left the thread of his discourse to tell a story that, from long experience, he knew would not fail to bring his listeners to a common feeling.

These things are important resources for the speaker, and happy is he who uses them worthily and not as a despicable charlatan. The difference between a demagogue and a leader is not so much a matter of method as of principle. Even the most dignified speaker must recognize the eternal laws of human nature. You are by no means urged to become a trickster on the platform far from it! but don't kill your speech with dignity. To be icily correct is as silly as to rant. Do neither, but appeal to those world-old elements in your audience that have been recognized by all great speakers from Demosthenes to Sam Small, and see to it that you never debase your powers by arousing your audience unworthily.

It is as hard to kindle enthusiasm in a scattered audience as to build a fire with scattered sticks. An audience to be converted into a crowd must be made to appear as a crowd. This cannot be done when they are widely scattered over a large seating space or when many empty benches separate the speaker from his listeners. Have your audience seated compactly. How many a preacher has bemoaned the enormous edifice over which what would normally be a large congregation has scattered in chilled and chilling solitude Sunday after Sunday! Bishop Brooks himself could not have inspired a congregation of one thousand souls seated in the vastness of St. Peter's at Rome. In that colossal sanctuary it is only on great occasions which bring out the multitudes that the service is before the high altar at other times the smaller side-chapels are used.

Universal ideas surcharged with feeling help to create the crowd-atmosphere. Examples: liberty, character, righteousness, courage, fraternity, altruism, country, and national heroes. George Cohan was making psychology practical and profitable when he introduced the flag and flag-songs into his musical comedies. Cromwell's regiments prayed before the battle and went into the fight singing hymns. The French corps, singing the Marseillaise in 1914, charged the Germans as one man. Such unifying devices arouse the feelings, make soldiers fanatical mobs and, alas, more efficient murderers.

□

26

Riding the Winged Horse

To think, and to feel, constitute the two grand divisions of men of genius—the men of reasoning and the men of imagination.

—ISAAC DISRAELI
Literary Character of Men of Genius

And as imagination bodies forth
The forms of things unknown, the poet's pen
Turns them to shapes and gives to airy nothing
A local habitation and a name.

—SHAKESPEARE
Midsummer-Night's Dream

It is common, among those who deal chiefly with life's practicalities, to think of imagination as having little value in comparison with direct thinking. They smile with tolerance when Emerson says that "Science does not know its debt to the imagination," for these are the words of a speculative essayist, a philosopher, a poet. But when Napoleon the indomitable welder of empires declares that "The human race is governed by its imagination," the authoritative word commands their respect.

Be it remembered, the faculty of forming *mental images* is

as efficient a cog as may be found in the whole mind-machine. True, it must fit into that other vital cog, pure thought, but when it does so it may be questioned which is the more productive of important results for the happiness and well-being of man. This should become more apparent as we go on.

I. What is Imagination?

Let us not seek for a definition, for a score of varying ones may be found, but let us grasp this fact: By imagination we mean either the faculty or the process of forming mental images.

The subject-matter of imagination may be really existent in nature, or not at all real, or a combination of both; it may be physical or spiritual, or both the mental image is at once the most lawless and the most law-abiding child that has ever been born of the mind.

First of all, as its name suggests, the process of imagination for we are thinking of it now as a process rather than as a faculty is memory at work. Therefore we must consider it primarily as

1. Reproductive Imagination

We see or hear or feel or taste or smell something and the sensation passes away. Yet we are conscious of a greater or lesser ability to reproduce such feelings at will. Two considerations, in general, will govern the vividness of the image thus evoked the strength of the original impression, and the reproductive power of one mind as compared with another. Yet every normal person will be able to evoke images with some degree of clearness.

The fact that not all minds possess this imaging faculty in anything like equal measure will have an important bearing on the public speaker's study of this question. No man who does not feel at least some poetic impulses is likely to aspire seriously to be a poet, yet many whose imaging faculties are so dormant as to seem actually dead do aspire to be public speakers. To all such we say most earnestly: Awaken your image-making gift, for even in the most coldly logical discourse it is sure to prove of great service. It is important that you find out at once just how full and how trustworthy is your imagination, for it is capable of cultivation as well as of abuse.

Francis Galton says: "The French appear to possess the visualising faculty in a high degree. The peculiar ability they show in pre-arranging ceremonials and fetes of all kinds and their undoubted genius for tactics and strategy show that they are able to foresee effects with unusual clearness. Their ingenuity in all technical contrivances is an additional testimony in the same direction, and so is their singular clearness of expression. Their phrase *figurez-vous, or picture to yourself*, seems to express their dominant mode of perception. Our equivalent, of 'image,' is ambiguous."

But individuals differ in this respect just as markedly as, for instance, the Dutch do from the French. And this is true not only of those who are classified by their friends as being respectively imaginative or unimaginative, but of those whose gifts or habits are not well known.

Let us take for experiment six of the best-known types of imaging and see in practice how they arise in our own minds.

By all odds the most common type is, (a) *the visual image*. Children who more readily recall things seen than things heard are called by psychologists "eye-minded," and most of us are bent in this direction. Close your eyes now and re-call the word thus hyphenated is more suggestive the scene around this morning's breakfast table. Possibly there was nothing striking in the situation and the image is therefore not striking. Then image any notable table scene in your experience how vividly it stands forth, because at the time you felt the impression strongly. Just then you may not have been conscious of how strongly the scene was laying hold upon you, for often we are so intent upon what we see that we give no particular thought to the fact that it is impressing us. It may surprise you to learn how accurately you are able to image a scene when a long time has elapsed between the conscious focussing of your attention on the image and the time when you saw the original.

(b) *The auditory image* is probably the next most vivid of our recalled experiences. Here association is potent to suggest similarities. Close out all the world beside and listen to the peculiar wood-against-wood sound of the sharp thunder among rocky mountains—the crash of ball against ten-pins may suggest it. Or image (the word is imperfect, for it seems to suggest only the eye) the sound of tearing ropes when some precious weight hangs in danger. Or recall the bay of a hound almost upon you in pursuit choose your own sound, and see how pleasantly or terribly real it becomes when imaged in your brain.

(c) *The motor image* is a close competitor with the auditory for second place. Have you ever awakened in the night, every muscle taut and striving, to feel your self straining against the opposing football line that held like a stone-wall or as firmly as the headboard of your bed? Or voluntarily recall the movement of the boat when you cried inwardly, "It's all up with me!" The perilous lurch of a train, the sudden sinking of an elevator, or the unexpected toppling of a rocking-chair may serve as further experiments.

(d) *The gustatory image* is common enough, as the idea of eating lemons will testify. Sometimes the pleasurable recollection of a delightful dinner will cause the mouth to water years afterward, or the "image" of particularly atrocious medicine will wrinkle the nose long after it made one day in boyhood wretched.

(e) *The olfactory image* is even more delicate. Some there are who are affected to illness by the memory of certain odours, while others experience the most delectable sensations by the rise of pleasing olfactory images.

(f) *The tactile image*, to name no others, is well nigh as potent. Do you shudder at the thought of velvet rubbed by short-nailed finger tips? Or were you ever "burned" by touching an ice-cold stove? Or, happier memory, can you still feel the touch of a well-loved absent hand?

Be it remembered that few of these images are present in our minds except in combination the sight and sound of the crashing avalanche are one; so are the flash and report of the huntman's gun that came so near "doing for us."

Thus, imaging especially conscious reproductive imagination will become a valuable part of our mental processes in proportion as we direct and control it.

2. Productive Imagination

All of the foregoing examples, and doubtless also many of the experiments you yourself may originate, are merely reproductive. Pleasurable or horrific as these may be, they are far less important than the images evoked by the productive imagination though that does not infer a separate faculty.

Recall, again for experiment, some scene whose beginning you once saw enacted on a streetcorner but passed by before the denouement was ready to be disclosed. Recall it all that far the image is reproductive. But what followed? Let your fantasy roam at pleasure, the succeeding scenes are productive, for you have more or less consciously invented the unreal on the basis of the real.

And just here the fictionist, the poet, and the public speaker will see the value of productive imagery. True, the feet of the idol you build are on the ground, but its head pierces the clouds, it is a son of both earth and heaven.

One fact it is important to note here: Imagery is a valuable mental asset in proportion as it is controlled by the higher intellectual power of pure reason. The untutored child of Nature thinks largely in images and therefore attaches to them undue importance. He readily confuses the real with the unreal to him they are of like value. But the man of training readily distinguishes the one from the other and evaluates each with some, if not with perfect, justice.

So we see that unrestrained imaging may produce a rudderless steamer, while the trained faculty is the graceful sloop, skimming the seas at her skipper's will, her course steadied by the helm of reason and her lightsome wings catching every air of heaven.

The game of chess, the war-lord's tactical plan, the evolution of a geometrical theorem, the devising of a great business campaign, the elimination of waste in a factory, the denouement of a powerful drama, the overcoming of an economic obstacle, the scheme for a sublime poem, and the convincing siege of an audience may nay, indeed must each be conceived in an image and wrought to reality according to the plans and specifications laid upon the trestle board by some modern imaginative Hiram. The farmer who would be content with the seed he possesses would have no harvest. Do not rest satisfied with the ability to recall images, but cultivate your creative imagination by building "what might be" upon the foundation of "what is."

II. The Uses of Imaging in Public Speaking

By this time you will have already made some general application of these ideas to the art of the platform, but to several specific uses we must now refer.

1. Imaging in Speech-Preparation

(a) *Set the image of your audience before you while you prepare.* Disappointment may lurk here, and you cannot be forearmed for every emergency, but in the main you must meet your audience before you actually do image its probable mood and attitude toward the occasion, the theme, and the speaker.

(b) *Conceive your speech as a whole while you are preparing its parts,* else can you not see image how its parts shall be fitly framed together.

(c) *Image the language you will use,* so far as written or

extemporaneous speech may dictate. The habit of imaging will give you choice of varied figures of speech, for remember that an address without *fresh* comparisons is like a garden without blooms. Do not be content with the first hackneyed figure that comes flowing to your pen-point, but dream on until the striking, the unusual, yet the vividly real comparison points your thought like steel does the arrow-tip.

Note the freshness and effectiveness of the following description from the opening of O. Henry's story, "The Harbinger."

Long before the springtide is felt in the dull bosom of the yokel does the city man know that the grass-green goddess is upon her throne. He sits at his breakfast eggs and toast, begirt by stone walls, opens his morning paper and sees journalism leave vernalism at the post.

For whereas Spring's couriers were once the evidence of our finer senses, now the Associated Press does the trick.

The warble of the first robin in Hackensack, the stirring of the maple sap in Bennington, the budding of the pussy willows along the main street in Syracuse, the first chirp of the blue bird, the swan song of the blue point, the annual tornado in St. Louis, the plaint of the peach pessimist from Pompton, N.J., the regular visit of the tame wild goose with a broken leg to the pond near Bilgewater Junction, the base attempt of the Drug Trust to boost the price of quinine foiled in the House by Congressman Jinks, the first tall poplar struck by lightning and the usual stunned picknickers who had taken refuge, the first crack of the ice jamb in the Allegheny River, the finding of a violet in its mossy bed by the correspondent at Round Corners, these are the advanced signs of the burgeoning season that are wired into the wise city, while the farmer sees nothing but winter upon his dreary fields.

But these be mere externals. The true harbinger is the heart. When Strephon seeks his Chloe and Mike his Maggie, then only is Spring arrived and the newspaper report of the five foot rattler killed in Squire Pettregrew's pasture confirmed.

A hackneyed writer would probably have said that the newspaper told the city man about spring before the farmer could see any evidence of it, but that the real harbinger of spring was love and that "In the Spring a young man's fancy lightly turns to thoughts of love."

2. Imaging in Speech-Delivery

When once the passion of speech is on you and you are "warmed up" perhaps by striking *till* the iron is hot so that you may not fail to strike *when* it is hot your mood will be one of vision.

Then (a) *Re-image past emotion* of which more elsewhere. The actor re-calls the old feelings every time he renders his telling lines.

(b) *Reconstruct in image the scenes you are to describe.*

(c) *Image the objects in nature whose tone you are delineating,* so that bearing and voice and movement (gesture) will picture forth the whole convincingly. Instead of merely stating the fact that whiskey ruins homes, the temperance speaker paints a drunkard coming home to abuse his wife and strike his children. It is much more effective than telling the truth in abstract terms. To depict the cruelness of war, do not assert the fact abstractly "War is cruel." Show the soldier, an arm swept away by a bursting shell, lying on the battlefield pleading for water; show the children with tear-stained faces pressed against the window pane praying for their dead father to return. Avoid general and prosaic terms. Paint pictures. Evolve images for the imagination of your audience to construct into pictures of their own.

III. How to Acquire the Imaging Habit

You remember the American statesman who asserted that "the way to resume is to resume"? The application is obvious.

Beginning with the first simple analyses of this chapter, test your own qualities of image-making. One by one practice the several kinds of images; then add even inventothers in combination, for many images come to us in complex form, like the combined noise and shoving and hot odour of a cheering crowd.

After practicing on reproductive imaging, turn to the productive, beginning with the reproductive and adding productive features for the sake of cultivating invention.

Frequently, allow your originating gifts full swing by weaving complete imaginary fabrics, sights, sounds, scenes; all the fine world of fantasy lies open to the journeyings of your winged steed.

In like manner train yourself in the use of figurative language. Learn first to distinguish and then to use its varied forms. *When used with restraint*, nothing can be more effective than the trope; but once let extravagance creep in by the window, and power will flee by the door.

All in all, master your images let not them master you.

□

27

Growing a Vocabulary

Boys flying kites haul in their white winged birds;
You can't do that way when you're flying words.
"Careful with fire," is good advice we know,
"Careful with words," is ten times doubly so.
Thoughts unexpressed many sometimes fall back dead;
But God Himself can't kill them when they're said.

—**WILL CARLETON**, *The First Settler's Story*

The term "vocabulary" has a special as well as a general meaning. True, *all* vocabularies are grounded in the everyday words of the language, out of which grow the special vocabularies, but each such specialised group possesses a number of words of peculiar value for its own objects. These words may be used in other vocabularies also, but the fact that they are suited to a unique order of expression marks them as of special value to a particular craft or calling.

In this respect the public speaker differs not at all from the poet, the novelist, the scientist, the traveller. He must add to his everyday stock, words of value for the public presentation of thought. "A study of the discourses of effective orators discloses the fact that they have a fondness for words signifying power, largeness, speed, action, colour, light, and all their opposites. They frequently employ words expressive of the various emotions. Descriptive words, adjectives used in *fresh* relations with nouns, and apt epithets, are freely employed. Indeed, the nature of public speech permits the use of mildly exaggerated words which, by the time they have reached the listener's judgment, will leave only a just impression"[J. Berg Esenwein].

Form the Book-Note Habit

To possess a word involves three things: To know its special and broader meanings, to know its relation to other words, and to be able to use it. When you see or hear a familiar word used in an unfamiliar sense, jot it down, look it up, and master it. We have in mind a speaker of superior attainments who acquired his vocabulary by noting all new words he heard or read. These he mastered and *put into use*. Soon his vocabulary became large, varied, and exact. Use a new word accurately five times and it is yours. Professor Albert E. Hancock says: "An author's vocabulary is of two kinds, latent and dynamic: latent those words he understands; dynamic those he can readily use. Every intelligent man *knows* all the words he needs, but he may not have them all ready for active service. The problem of literary diction consists in turning the latent into the dynamic." Your dynamic vocabulary is the one you must especially cultivate.

In his essay on "A College Magazine" in the volume, *Memories and Portraits*, Stevenson shows how he rose from imitation to originality in the use of words. He had particular reference to the formation of his literary style, but words are the raw materials of style, and his excellent example may well be followed judiciously by the public speaker. Words *in their relations* are vastly more important than words considered singly.

"Whenever I read a book or a passage that particularly pleased me, in which a thing was said or an effect rendered with propriety, in which there was either some conspicuous force or some happy distinction in the style, I must sit down at once and set myself to ape that quality. I was unsuccessful, and I knew it; and tried again, and was again unsuccessful, and always unsuccessful; but at least in these vain bouts I got some practice in rhythm, in harmony, in construction and coordination of parts.

I have thus played the sedulous ape to Hazlitt, to Lamb, to Wordsworth, to Sir Thomas Browne, to Defoe, to Hawthorne, to Montaigne.

That, like it or not, is the way to learn to write; whether I have profited or not, that is the way. It was the way Keats learned, and there never was a finer temperament for literature than Keats'.

It is the great point of these imitations that there still shines beyond the student's reach, his inimitable model. Let him try as he please, he is still sure of failure; and it is an old and very true saying that failure is the only highroad to success."

Form the Reference-Book Habit

Do not be content with your general knowledge of a word—press your study until you have mastered its individual shades of meaning and usage. Mere fluency is sure to become despicable, but accuracy never. The dictionary contains the crystallized usage of intellectual giants. No one who would write effectively dare despise its definitions and discriminations. Think, for example, of the different meanings of *mantle*, or *model*, or *quantity*. Any late edition of an unabridged dictionary is good, and is worth making sacrifices to own.

Books of synonyms and antonyms used cautiously, for there are few *perfect* synonyms in any language will be found of great help. Consider the shades of meanings among such word-groups as *thief*, peculator, defaulter, embezzler, burglar, yeggman, robber, bandit, marauder, *pirate*, and many more; or the distinctions among *Hebrew, Jew, Israelite, and Semite*.

Remember that no book of synonyms is trustworthy unless used with a dictionary. "A Thesaurus of the English Language," by Dr. Francis A. March, is expensive, but full and authoritative. Of smaller books of synonyms and antonyms there are plenty.

Study the connectives of English speech. Unsuspected pitfalls lie in the loose use *of and, or, for, while,* and a score of tricky little connectives.

Word derivations are rich in suggestiveness. Our English owes so much to foreign tongues and has changed so much with the centuries that whole addresses may grow out of a single root-idea hidden away in an ancient word-origin. Translation, also, is excellent exercise in word-mastery and consorts well with the study of derivations.

Phrase books that show the origins of familiar expressions will surprise most of us by showing how carelessly everyday speech is used.

A prefix or a suffix may essentially change the force of the stem, as in *master-ful* and *masterly, contempt-ible* and *contempt-uous, envi-ous* and *envi-able.* Thus to study words in groups, according to their stems, prefixes, and suffixes is to gain a mastery over their shades of meaning, and introduce us to other related words.

Do not Favour one Set or Kind of Words more than Another

"Sixty years and more ago, Lord Brougham, addressing the students of the University of Glasgow, laid down the rule that the native (Anglo-Saxon) part of our vocabulary was to be favoured at the expence of that other part which has come from the Latin and Greek. The rule was an impossible one, and Lord Brougham himself never tried seriously to observe it; nor, in truth, has any great writer made the attempt. Not only is our language highly composite, but the component words have, in De Quincey's phrase, 'happily coalesced.' It is easy to jest at words in *osity* and *-ation*, as 'dictionary' words, and the like. But even Lord Brougham would have found it difficult to dispense with *pomposity* and *imagination*."

The short, vigorous Anglo-Saxon will always be preferred for passages of special thrust and force, just as the Latin will continue to furnish us with flowing and smooth expressions; to mingle all sorts, however, will give variety and that is most to be desired.

Discuss Words With Those Who Know Them

Since the language of the platform follows closely the diction of everyday speech, many useful words may be acquired in conversation with cultivated men, and when such discussion takes the form of disputation as to the meanings and usages of words, it will prove doubly valuable. The development of word-power marches with the growth of individuality.

Search Faithfully for the Right Word

Books of reference are tripled in value when their owner has a passion for getting the kernels out of their shells. Ten minutes a day will do wonders for the nut-cracker. "I am growing so peevish about my writing," says Flaubert. "I am like a man whose ear is true, but who plays falsely on the violin: his fingers refuse to reproduce precisely those sounds of which he has the inward sense. Then the tears come rolling down from the poor scraper's eyes and the bow falls from his hand."

The same brilliant Frenchman sent this sound advice to his pupil, Guy de Maupassant: "Whatever may be the thing which one wishes to say, there is but one word for expressing it, only one verb to animate it, only one adjective to qualify it. It is essential to search for this word, for this verb, for this adjective, until they are discovered, and to be satisfied with nothing else."

Walter Savage Landor once wrote: "I hate false words, and seek with care, difficulty, and moroseness those that fit the thing." So did Sentimental Tommy, as related by James M. Barrie in his novel bearing his hero's name as a title. No wonder T. Sandys became an author and a lion!

Tommy, with another lad, is writing an essay on "A Day in Church," in competition for a university scholarship. He gets on finely until he pauses for lack of a word. For nearly an hour he searches for this elusive thing, until suddenly he is told that the allotted time is up, and he has lost! Barrie may tell the rest:

Essay! It was no more an essay than a twig is a tree, for the gowk had stuck in the middle of his second page. Yes, stuck is the right expression, as his chagrined teacher had to admit when the boy was cross-examined. He had not been "up to some of his tricks;" he had stuck, and his explanations, as you will admit, merely emphasized his incapacity.

He had brought himself to public scorn for lack of a word. What word? they asked testily; but even now he could not tell. He had wanted a Scotch word that would signify how many people were in Church, and it was on the tip of his tongue, but would come no farther. Puckle was nearly the word, but it did not mean so many people as he meant. The hour had gone by just like winking; he had forgotten all about time while searching his mind for the word.

*****

The other five [examiners] were furious.... "You little tattie doolie," Cathro roared, "were there not a dozen words to wile from if you had an ill-will to puckle? What ailed you at manzy, or"

"I thought of manzy," replied Tommy, woefully, for he was ashamed of himself, "but—but a manzy's a swarm. It would mean that the folk in the kirk were buzzing thegither like bees, instead of sitting still."

"Even if it does mean that," said Mr. Duthie, with impatience, "what was the need of being so particular? Surely the art of essay-writing consists in using the first word that comes and hurrying on."

"That's how I did," said the proud McLauchlan [Tommy's successful competitor]....

"I see," interposed Mr. Gloag, "that McLauchlan speaks of there being a mask of people in the Church. Mask is a fine Scotch word."

"I thought of mask," whimpered Tommy, "but that would mean the kirk was crammed, and I just meant it to be middling full."

"Flow would have done," suggested Mr. Lonimer.

"Flow's but a handful," said Tommy.

"Curran, then, you jackanapes!"

"Curran's no enough."

Mr. Lorrimer flung up his hands in despair.

"I wanted something between curran and mask," said Tommy, doggedly, yet almost at the crying.

Mr. Ogilvy, who had been hiding his admiration with difficulty, spread a net for him. "You said you wanted a word that meant middling full. Well, why did you not say middling full or fell mask?"

"Yes, why not?" demanded the ministers, unconsciously caught in the net.

"I wanted one word," replied Tommy, unconsciously avoiding it.

"You jewel!" muttered Mr. Ogilvy under his breath, but Mr. Cathro would have banged the boy's head had not the ministers interfered.

"It is so easy, too, to find the right word," said Mr. Gloag.

"It's no; it's difficult as to hit a squirrel," cried Tommy, and again Mr. Ogilvy nodded approval.

*****

And then an odd thing happened. As they were preparing

to leave the school [Cathro having previously run Tommy out by the neck], the door opened a little and there appeared in the aperture the face of Tommy, tear-stained but excited. "I ken the word now," he cried, "it came to me a' at once; it is hantle!"

Mr. Ogilvy ... said in an ecstasy to himself, "He *had* to think of it till he got it and he got it. The laddie is a genius!"

□

28

Memory Training

Lulled in the countless chambers of the brain,
Our thoughts are linked by many a hidden chain;
Awake but one, and lo! what myriads rise!
Each stamps its image as the other flies!

*****

Hail, memory, hail! in thy exhaustless mine
From age to age unnumber'd treasures shine!
Thought and her shadowy brood thy call obey,
And Place and Time are subject to thy sway!

—**SAMUEL ROGERS**, *Pleasures of Memory*

Many an orator, like Thackeray, has made the best part of his speech to himself on the way home from the lecture hall. Presence of mind it remained for Mark Twain to observe is greatly promoted by absence of body. A hole in the memory is no less a common complaint than a distressing one.

Henry Ward Beecher was able to deliver one of the world's greatest addresses at Liverpool because of his excellent memory. In speaking of the occasion Mr. Beecher said that all the events, arguments and appeals that he had ever heard or read or written seemed to pass before his mind as oratorical weapons, and standing there he had but to reach forth his hand and "seize the weapons as they went smoking by." Ben Jonson could repeat all he had written. Scaliger memorised the Iliad in three weeks. Locke says: "Without memory, man is a perpetual infant." Quintilian and Aristotle regarded it as a measure of genius.

Now all this is very good. We all agree that a reliable memory is an invaluable possession for the speaker. We never dissent for a moment when we are solemnly told that his memory should be a storehouse from which at pleasure he can draw facts, fancies, and illustrations. But can the memory be trained to act as the warder for all the truths that we have gained from thinking, reading, and experience? And if so, how? Let us see.

Twenty years ago a poor immigrant boy, employed as a dish washer in New York, wandered into the Cooper Union and began to read a copy of Henry George's "Progress and Poverty." His passion for knowledge was awakened, and he became a habitual reader. But he found that he was not able to remember what he read, so he began to train his naturally poor memory until he became the world's greatest memory expert. This man was the late Mr. Felix Berol. Mr. Berol could tell the population of any town in the world, of more than five thousand inhabitants. He could recall the names of forty strangers who had just been introduced to him and was able to tell which had been presented third, eighth, seventeenth, or in any order. He knew the date of every important event in history, and could not only recall an endless array of facts but could correlate them perfectly.

To what extent Mr. Berol's remarkable memory was natural and required only attention, for its development, seems impossible to determine with exactness, but the evidence clearly indicates that, however useless were many of his memory feats, a highly retentive memory was developed where before only "a good forgettery" existed.

The freak memory is not worth striving for, but a good working memory decidedly is. Your power as a speaker will depend to a large extent upon your ability to retain impressions and call them forth when occasion demands, and that sort of memory is like muscle it responds to training.

What Not to Do

It is sheer misdirected effort to begin to memorise by learning words by rote, for that is beginning to build a pyramid at the apex. For years our schools were cursed by this vicious system vicious not only because it is inefficient but for the more important reason that it hurts the mind. True, some minds are natively endowed with a wonderful facility in remembering strings of words, facts, and figures, but such are rarely good reasoning minds; the normal person must belabour and force the memory to acquire in this artificial way.

Again, it is hurtful to force the memory in hours of physical weakness or mental weariness. Health is the basis of the best mental action and the operation of memory is no exception.

Finally, do not become a slave to a system. Knowledge of a few simple facts of mind and memory will set you to work at the right end of the operation. Use these *principles*, whether included in a system or not, but do not bind yourself to a method that tends to lay more stress on the *way* to remember than on the development of memory itself. It is nothing short of ridiculous to memorise ten words in order to remember one fact.

The Natural Laws of Memory

Concentrated attention at the time when you wish to store the mind is the first step in memorizing and the most important one by far. You forgot the fourth of the list of articles your wife asked you to bring home chiefly because you allowed your attention to waver for an instant when she was telling you. Attention may not be concentrated attention. When a siphon is charged with gas it is sufficiently filled with the carbonic acid vapour to make its influence felt; a mind charged with an idea is charged to a degree sufficient to hold it. Too much charging will make the siphon burst; too much attention to trifles leads to insanity. Adequate attention, then, is the fundamental secret of remembering.

Generally we do not give a fact adequate attention when it does not seem important. Almost everyone has seen how the seeds in an apple point, and has memorised the date of Washington's death. Most of us have perhaps wisely forgotten both. The little nick in the bark of a tree is healed over and obliterated in a season, but the gashes in the trees around Gettysburg are still apparent after fifty years. Impressions that are gathered lightly are soon obliterated. Only deep impressions can be recalled at will. Henry Ward Beecher said: "One intense hour will do more than dreamy years." To memorise ideas and words, concentrate on them until they are fixed firmly and deeply in your mind and accord to them their true importance. LISTEN with the mind and you will remember.

How shall you concentrate? How would you increase the fighting-effectiveness of a man-of-war? One vital way would be to increase the size and number of its guns. To strengthen your memory, increase both the number and the force of your mental impressions by attending to them intensely. Loose, skimming reading, and drifting habits of reading destroy memory power. However, as most books and newspapers do not warrant any other kind of attention, it will not do altogether to condemn this method of reading; but avoid it when you are trying to memorise.

Environment has a strong influence upon concentration, until you have learned to be alone in a crowd and undisturbed by clamour. When you set out to memorise a fact or a speech, you may find the task easier away from all sounds and moving objects. All impressions foreign to the one you desire to fix in your mind must be eliminated.

The next great step in memorizing is to *pick out the essentials of the subject*, arrange them in order, and dwell upon them intently. Think clearly of each essential, one after the other.

Thinking a thing not allowing the mind to wander to non-essentials—is really memorizing.

Association of ideas is universally recognized as an essential in memory work; indeed, whole systems of memory training have been founded on this principle.

Many speakers memorise only the outlines of their addresses, filling in the words at the moment of speaking. Some have found it helpful to remember an outline by associating the different points with objects in the room. Speaking on "Peace," you may wish to dwell on the cost, the cruelty, and the failure of war, and so lead to the justice of arbitration. Before going on the platform if you will associate four divisions of your outline with four objects in the room, this association may help you to recall them. You may be prone to forget your third point, but you remember that once when you were speaking the electric lights failed, so arbitrarily the electric light globe will help you to remember "failure." Such associations, being unique, tend to stick in the mind. While recently speaking on the six kinds of imagination the present writer formed them into an acrostic *visual*, *auditory*, *motor*, *gustatory*, *olfactory*, and *tactile*, furnished the nonsense word *vamgot*, but the six points were easily remembered.

In the same way that children are taught to remember the spelling of teasing words *separate* comes from *separ* and as an automobile driver remembers that two C's and then two H's lead him into Castor Road, Cottman Street, Haynes Street and Henry Street, so important points in your address may be fixed in mind by arbitrary symbols invented by yourself. The very work of devising the scheme is a memory action. The psychological process is simple: it is one of noting intently the steps by which a fact, or a truth, or even a word, has come to you. Take advantage of this tendency of the mind to remember by association.

Repetition is a powerful aid to memory. Thurlow Weed, the journalist and political leader, was troubled because he so easily forgot the names of persons he met from day-to-day. He corrected the weakness, relates Professor William James, by forming the habit of attending carefully to names he had heard during the day and then repeating them to his wife every evening. Doubtless Mrs. Weed was heroically longsuffering, but the device worked admirably.

After reading a passage you would remember, close the book, reflect, and repeat the contents aloud, if possible.

Reading thoughtfully aloud has been found by many to be a helpful memory practice.

Write what you wish to remember. This is simply one more way of increasing the number and the strength of your mental impressions by utilising *all* your avenues of impression. It will help to fix a speech in your mind if you speak it aloud, listen to it, write it out, and look at it intently. You have then impressed it on your mind by means of vocal, auditory, muscular and visual impressions.

Some folk have peculiarly distinct auditory memories; they are able to recall things heard much better than things seen. Others have the visual memory; they are best able to recall sight-impressions. As you recall a walk you have taken, are you able to remember better the sights or the sounds? Find out what kinds of impressions your memory retains best, and use them the most. To fix an idea in mind, use *every* possible kind of impression.

Daily habit is a great memory cultivator. Learn a lesson from the Marathon runner. Regular exercise, though never so little daily, will strengthen your memory in a surprising measure. Try to describe in detail the dress, looks and manner of the people you pass on the street. Observe the room you are in, close your eyes, and describe its contents. View closely the landscape, and write out a detailed description of it. How much did you miss? Notice the contents of the show windows on the street; how many features are you able to recall? Continual practice in this feat may develop in you as remarkable proficiency as it did in Robert Houdin and his son.

The daily memorizing of a beautiful passage in literature will not only lend strength to the memory, but will store the mind with gems for quotation. But whether by little or much add daily to your memory power by practice.

Memorize out of doors. The buoyancy of the wood, the shore, or the stormy night on deserted streets may freshen your mind as it does the minds of countless others.

Lastly, *cast out fear*. Tell yourself that you *can* and *will* and *do* remember. By pure exercise of selfism assert your mastery. Be obsessed with the fear of forgetting and you cannot remember. Practice the reverse. Throw aside your manuscript crutches you may tumble once or twice, but what matters that, for you are going to learn to walk and leap and run.

Memorizing a Speech

Now let us try to put into practice the foregoing suggestions. First, re-read this chapter, noting the nine ways by which memorizing may be helped.

Then read over a selection applying so many of the suggestions as are practicable. Get the spirit of the selection firmly in your mind. Make mental note of write down, if you must the *succession* of ideas. Now memorise the thought. Then memorise the outline, the order in which the different ideas are expressed. Finally, memorise the exact wording.

No, when you have done all this, with the most faithful attention to directions, you will not find memorizing easy, unless you have previously trained your memory, or it is naturally retentive. Only by constant practice will memory become strong and only by continually observing these same principles will it remain strong. You will, however, have made a beginning, and that is no mean matter.

In Case of Trouble

But what are you to do if, notwithstanding all your efforts, you should forget your points, and your mind, for the minute, becomes blank? This is a deplorable condition that sometimes arises and must be dealt with. Obviously, you can sit down and admit defeat. Such a consummation is devoutly to be shunned.

Walking slowly across the platform may give you time to grip yourself, compose your thoughts, and stave off disaster. Perhaps the surest and most practical method is to begin a new sentence with your last important word. This is not advocated as a method of composing a speech it is merely an extreme measure which may save you in tight circumstances. It is like the fire department the less you must use it the better. If this method is followed very long you are likely to find yourself talking about plum pudding or Chinese Gordon in the most unexpected manner, so of course you will get back to your lines the earliest moment that your feet have hit the platform.

Let us see how this plan works obviously, your extemporised words will lack somewhat of polish, but in such a pass crudity is better than failure.

Now you have come to a dead wall after saying: "Joan of Arc fought for liberty." By this method you might get something like this:

"Liberty is a sacred privilege for which mankind always had to fight. These struggles [Platitude but push on] fill the pages of history. History records the gradual triumph of the serf over the lord, the slave over the master. The master has continually tried to usurp unlimited powers. Power during the medieval ages accrued to the owner of the land with a spear and a strong castle; but the strong castle and spear were of little avail after the discovery of gunpowder. Gunpowder was the greatest boon that liberty had ever known."

Thus far you have linked one idea with another rather obviously, but you are getting your second wind now and may venture to relax your grip on the too-evident chain; and so you say:

"With gunpowder the humblest serf in all the land could put an end to the life of the tyrannical baron behind the castle walls. The struggle for liberty, with gunpowder as its aid, wrecked empires, and built up a new era for all mankind."

In a moment more you have gotten back to your outline and the day is saved.

Practicing exercises like the above will not only fortify you against the death of your speech when your memory misses fire, but it will also provide an excellent training for fluency in speaking. *Stock up with ideas.*

□

29

Right Thinking and Personality

Whatever crushes individuality is despotism, by whatever name it may be called.
—**JOHN STUART MILL**, *On Liberty*

Right thinking fits for complete living by developing the power to appreciate the beautiful in nature and art, power to think the true and to will the good, power to live the life of thought, and faith, and hope, and love.
—**N.C. SCHAEFFER**
Thinking and Learning to Think

The speaker's most valuable possession is personality that indefinable, imponderable something which sums up what we are, and makes us different from others; that distinctive force of self which operates appreciably on those whose lives we touch. It is personality alone that makes us long for higher things. Rob us of our sense of individual life, with its gains and losses, its duties and joys, and we grovel. "Few human creatures," says John Stuart Mill, "would consent to be changed into any of the lower animals for a promise of the fullest allowance of a beast's pleasures; no intelligent human being would consent to be a fool, no instructed person would be an ignoramus, no person of feeling and conscience would be selfish and base, even though he should be persuaded that the fool, or the dunce, or the rascal is better satisfied with his lot than they with theirs.... It is better to be a human being dissatisfied than a pig satisfied, better to be a Socrates dissatisfied than a fool satisfied. And if the fool or the pig is of a different opinion, it is only because they know only their own side of the question. The other party to the comparison knows both sides."

Now it is precisely because the Socrates type of person lives on the plan of right thinking and restrained feeling and willing that he prefers his state to that of the animal. All that a man is, all his happiness, his sorrow, his achievements, his failures, his magnetism, his weakness, all are in an amazingly large measure the direct results of his thinking. Thought and heart combine to produce *right* thinking: "As a man thinketh in his heart so is he." As he does not think in his heart so he can never become.

Since this is true, personality can be developed and its latent powers broughtout by careful cultivation. We have long since ceased to believe that we are living in a realm of chance. So clear and exact are Nature's laws that we forecast, scores of years in advance, the appearance of a certain comet and foretell to the minute an eclipse of the Sun. And we understand this law of cause and effect in all our material realms. We do not plant potatoes and expect to pluck hyacinths. The law is universal: it applies to our mental powers, to morality, to personality, quite as much as to the heavenly bodies and the grain of the fields. "Whatsoever a man soweth that shall he also reap," and nothing else.

Character has always been regarded as one of the chief factors of the speaker's power. Cato defined the orator as *vir bonus dicendi peritus* a good man skilled in speaking. Phillips Brooks says: "Nobody can truly stand as a utterer before the world, unless he be profoundly living and earnestly thinking." "Character," says Emerson, "is a natural power, like light and heat, and all nature cooperates with it. The reason why we feel one man's presence, and do not feel another's is as simple as gravity. Truth is the summit of being: justice is the application of it to affairs. All individual natures stand in a scale, according to the purity of this element in them. The will of the pure runs down into other natures, as water runs down from a higher into a lower vessel. This natural force is no more to be withstood than any other natural force.... Character is nature in the highest form."

It is absolutely impossible for impure, bestial and selfish thoughts to blossom into loving and altruistic habits. Thistle seeds bring forth only the thistle. Contrariwise, it is entirely impossible for continual altruistic, sympathetic, and serviceful thoughts to bring forth a low and vicious character. Either thoughts or feelings precede and determine all our actions. Actions develop into habits, habits constitute character, and character determines destiny. Therefore to guard our thoughts and control our feelings is to shape our destinies. The syllogism is complete, and old as it is it is still true.

Since "character is nature in the highest form," the development of character must proceed on natural lines. The garden left to itself will bring forth weeds and scrawny plants, but the flower-beds nurtured carefully will blossom into fragrance and beauty.

As the student entering college largely determines his vocation by choosing from the different courses of the curriculum, so do we choose our characters by choosing our thoughts. We are steadily going up toward that which we most wish for, or steadily sinking to the level of our low desires. What we secretly cherish in our hearts is a symbol of what we shall receive. Our trains of thoughts are hurrying us on to our destiny. When you see the flag fluttering to the South, you know the wind is coming from the North. When you see the straws and papers being carried to the Northward you realize the wind is blowing out of the South. It is just as easy to ascertain a man's thoughts by observing the tendency of his character.

Let it not be suspected for one moment that all this is merely a preachment on the question of morals. It is that, but much more, for it touches the whole man his imaginative nature, his ability to control his feelings, the mastery of his thinking faculties, and perhaps most largely his power to will and to carry his volitions into effective action.

Right thinking constantly assumes that the will sits enthroned to execute the dictates of mind, conscience and heart. *Never tolerate for an instant the suggestion thut your will is not absolutely efficient.* The way to will is to will and the very first time you are tempted to break a worthy resolution and you will be, you may be certain of that *make your fight then and there*. You cannot afford to lose that fight. *You must* win, it don't swerve for an instant, but keep that resolution if it kills you. It will not, but you must fight just as though life depended on the victory; and indeed your personality may actually lie in the balances!

Your success or failure as a speaker will be determined very largely by your thoughts and your mental attitude. The present writer had a student of limited education enter one of his classes in public speaking. He proved to be a very poor speaker; and the instructor could conscientiously do little but point out faults. However, the young man was warned not to be discouraged. With sorrow in his voice and the essence of earnestness beaming from his eyes, he replied: "I will not be discouraged! I want so badly to know how to speak!" It was warm, human, and from the very heart. And he did keep on trying and developed into a creditable speaker.

There is no power under the stars that can defeat a man with that attitude. He who down in the deeps of his heart earnestly longs to get facility in speaking, and is willing to make the sacrifices necessary, will reach his goal. "Ask and ye shall receive; seek and ye shall find; knock and it shall be opened unto you," is indeed applicable to those who would acquire speech-power. You will not realize the prize that you wish for languidly, but the goal that you start out to attain with the spirit of the old guard that dies but never surrenders, you will surely reach.

Your belief in your ability and your willingness to make sacrifices for that belief, are the double index to your future achievements. Lincoln had a dream of his possibilities as a speaker. He transmuted that dream into life solely because he walked many miles to borrow books which he read by the log-fire glow at night. He sacrificed much to realize his vision. Livingstone had a great faith in his ability to serve the benighted races of Africa. To actualize that faith he gave up all. Leaving England for the interior of the Dark Continent he struck the death blow to Europe's profits from the slave trade. Joan of Arc had great self-confidence, glorified by an infinite capacity for sacrifice. She drove the English beyond the Loire, and stood beside Charles while he was crowned.

These all realized their strongest desires. The law is universal. Desire greatly, and you shall achieve; sacrifice much, and you shall obtain.

Stanton Davis Kirkham has beautifully expressed this thought: "You may be keeping accounts, and presently you shall walk out of the door that has for so long seemed to you the barrier of your ideals, and shall find yourself before an audience, the pen still behind your ear, the ink stains on your fingers—and then and there shall pour out the torrent of your inspiration. You may be driving sheep, and you shall wander to the city, bucolic and open-mouthed; shall wander under the intrepid guidance of the spirit into the studio of the master, and after a time he shall say, I have nothing more to teach you.' And now you have become the master, who did so recently dream of great things while driving sheep. You shall lay down the saw and the plane to take upon yourself the regeneration of the world."

□

30

After-dinner and other Occasional Speaking

The perception of the ludicrous is a pledge of sanity.

—**RALPH WALDO EMERSON**, *Essays*

And let him be sure to leave other men their turns to speak.

—**FRANCIS BACON**
Essay on *Civil and Moral Discourse*

Perhaps the most brilliant, and certainly the most entertaining, of all speeches are those delivered on after-dinner and other special occasions. The air of well-fed content in the former, and of expectancy well primed in the latter, furnishes an audience which, though not readily won, is prepared for the best, while the speaker himself is pretty sure to have been chosen for his gifts of oratory.

The first essential of good occasional speaking is to study the occasion. Precisely what is the object of the meeting? How important is the occasion to the audience? How large will the audience be? What sort of people are they? How large is the auditorium? Who selects the speakers' themes? Who else is to speak? What are they to speak about? Precisely how long am

I to speak? Who speaks before I do and who follows?

If you want to hit the nail on the head ask such questions as these. No occasional address can succeed unless it fits the occasion to a Many prominent men have lost prestige because they were too careless or too busy or too self-confident to respect the occasion and the audience by learning the exact conditions under which they were to speak. Leaving *too* much to the moment is taking a long chance and generally means a less effective speech, if not a failure.

Suitability is the big thing in an occasional speech. When Mark Twain addressed the Army of the Tennessee in reunion at Chicago, in 1877, he responded to the toast, "The Babies." Two things in that after dinner speech are remarkable: the bright introduction, by which he subtly *claimed* the interest of all, and the humorous use of military terms throughout:

"Mr. Chairman and Gentlemen: "The Babies." Now, that's something like. We haven't all had the good fortune to be ladies; we have not all been generals, or poets, or statesmen; but when the toast works down to the babies, we stand on common ground for we've all been babies. It is a shame that for a thousand years the world's banquets have utterly ignored the baby, as if he didn't amount to anything! If you, gentlemen, will stop and think a minute if you will go back fifty or a hundred years, to your early married life, and recontemplate your first baby you will remember that he amounted to a good deal and even something over."

"As a vessel is known by the sound, whether it be cracked or not," said Demosthenes, "so men are proved by their speeches whether they be wise or foolish." Surely the occasional address furnishes a severe test of a speaker's wisdom. To be trivial on a serious occasion, to be funereal at a banquet, to be long-winded ever these are the marks of nonsense. Some imprudent souls seem to select the most friendly of after-dinner occasions for the explosion of a bomb-shell of dispute. Around the dinner table it is the custom of even political enemies to bury their hatchets anywhere rather than in some convenient skull. It is the height of bad taste to raise questions that in hours consecrated to good-will can only irritate.

Occasional speeches offer good chances for humour, particularly the funny story, for humour with a genuine point is not trivial. But do not spin a whole skein of humorous yarns with no more connection than the inane and threadbare "And that reminds me." An anecdote without bearing may be funny but one less funny that fits theme and occasion is far preferable. There is no way, short of sheer power of speech, that so surely leads to the heart of an audience as rich, appropriate humour. The scattered diners in a great banqueting hall, the after-dinner lethargy, the anxiety over approaching last-train time, the over-full list of over-full speakers all throw out a challenge to the speaker to do his best to win an interested hearing. And when success does come it is usually due to a happy mixture of seriousness and humour, for humour alone rarely scores so heavily as the two combined, while the utterly grave speech *never* does on such occasions.

If there is one place more than another where second-hand opinions and platitudes are unwelcome it is in the after-dinner speech. Whether you are toast-master or the last speaker to try to hold the waning crowd at midnight, be as original as you can.

Commemorative occasions, unveilings, commencements, dedications, eulogies, and all the train of special public gatherings, offer rare opportunities for the display of tact and good sense in handling occasion, theme, and audience. When to be dignified and when colloquial, when to soar and when to ramble arm in arm with your listeners, when to flame and when to soothe, when to instruct and when to amuse in a word, the whole matter of APPROPRIATENESS must constantly be in mind lest you write your speech on water.

Finally, remember the beatitude: Blessed is the man that maketh short speeches, for he shall be invited to speak again.

□

31

Making Conversation Effective

In conversation avoid the extremes of forwardness and reserve.

—CATO

Conversation is the laboratory and workshop of the student.

—EMERSON, *Essays: Circles*

The father of W.E. Gladstone considered conversation to be both an art and an accomplishment. Around the dinner table in his home some topic of local or national interest, or some debated question, was constantly being discussed. In this way a friendly rivalry for supremacy in conversation arose among the family, and an incident observed in the street, an idea gleaned from a book, a deduction from personal experience, was carefully stored as material for the family exchange. Thus his early years of practice in elegant conversation prepared the younger Gladstone for his career as a leader and speaker.

There is a sense in which the ability to converse effectively is efficient public speaking, for our conversation is often heard by many, and occasionally decisions of great moment hinge upon the tone and quality of what we say in private.

Indeed, conversation in the aggregate probably wields

more power than press and platform combined. Socrates taught his great truths, not from public rostrums, but in personal converse. Men-made pilgrimages to Goethe's library and Coleridge's home to be charmed and instructed by their speech, and the culture of many nations was immeasurably influenced by the thoughts that streamed out from those rich well-springs.

Most of the world-moving speeches are made in the course of conversation. Conferences of diplomats, business-getting arguments, decisions by boards of directors, considerations of corporate policy, all of which influence the political, mercantile and economic maps of the world, are usually the results of careful though informal conversation, and the man whose opinions weigh in such crises is he who has first carefully pondered the words of both antagonist and protagonist.

However important it may be to attain self-control in light social converse, or about the family table, it is undeniably vital to have oneself perfectly in hand while taking part in a momentous conference. Then the hints that we have given on poise, alertness, precision of word, clearness of statement, and force of utterance, with respect to public speech, are equally applicable to conversation.

The form of nervous egotism for it is both that suddenly ends in flusters just when the vital words need to be uttered, is the sign of coming defeat, for a conversation is often a contest. If you feel this tendency embarrassing you, be sure to listen to Holmes's advice:

> And when you stick on conversational burs,
> Don't strew your pathway with those dreadful *urs*.

Here bring your will into action, for your trouble is a wandering attention. You must *force* your mind to persist along the chosen line of conversation and resolutely refuse to be diverted by *any* subject or happening that may unexpectedly pop up to distract you. To fail here is to lose effectiveness utterly.

Concentration is the keynote of conversational charm and efficiency. The haphazard habit of expression that uses bird-shot when a bullet is needed insures missing the game, for diplomacy of all sorts rests upon the precise application of precise words, particularly if one may paraphrase Tallyrand in those crises when language is no longer used to conceal thought.

We may frequently gain new light on old subjects by looking at word-derivations. Conversation signifies in the original a turn-about exchange of ideas, yet most people seem to regard it as a monologue. Bronson Alcott used to say that many could argue, but few converse. The first thing to remember in conversation, then, is that listening respectful, sympathetic, alert listening is not only due to our fellow converser but due to ourselves. Many a reply loses its point because the speaker is so much interested in what he is about to say that it is really no reply at all but merely an irritating and humiliating irrelevancy.

Self-expression is exhilarating. This explains the eternal impulse to decorate totem poles and paint pictures, write poetry and expound philosophy. One of the chief delights of conversation is the opportunity it affords for self-expression. A good conversationalist who monopolizes all the conversation, will be voted a bore because he denies others the enjoyment of self-expression, while a mediocre talker who listens interestedly may be considered a good conversationalist because he permits his companions to please themselves through self-expression. They are praised who please: they please who listen well.

The first step in remedying habits of confusion in manner, awkward bearing, vagueness in thought, and lack of precision in utterance, is to recognize your faults. If you are serenely unconscious of them, no one least of all yourself can help you. But once diagnose your own weaknesses, and you can overcome them by doing four things:

1. *WILL* to overcome them, and keep on willing.
2. Hold yourself in hand by assuring yourself that you

know precisely what you ought to say. If you cannot do that, be quiet until you are clear on this vital point.

3. Having thus assured yourself, cast out the fear of those who listen to you they are only human and will respect your words if you really have something to say and say it briefly, simply, and clearly.
4. Have the courage to study the English language until you are master of at least its simpler forms.

Conversational Hints

Choose some subject that will prove of general interest to the whole group. Do not explain the mechanism of a gas engine at an afternoon tea or the culture of hollyhocks at a stag party.

It is not considered good taste for a man to bare his arm in public and show scars or deformities. It is equally bad form for him to flaunt his own woes, or the deformity of some one else's character. The public demands plays and stories that end happily. All the world is seeking happiness. They cannot long be interested in your ills and troubles. George Cohan made himself a millionaire before he was thirty by writing cheerful plays. One of his rules is generally applicable to conversation: "Always leave them laughing when you say good-bye."

Dynamite the "I" out of your conversation. Not one man in nine hundred and seven can talk about himself without being a bore. The man who can perform that feat can achieve marvels without talking about himself, so the eternal "I" is not permissible even in his talk.

If you habitually build your conversation around your own interests it may prove very tiresome to your listener. He may be thinking of bird dogs or dry fly fishing while you are discussing the fourth dimension, or the merits of a cucumber lotion. The charming conversationalist is prepared to talk in terms of his listener's interest. If his listener spends his spare time investigating Guernsey cattle or agitating social reforms, the discriminating conversationalist shapes his remarks accordingly. A man of mediocre ability can charm men much abler than himself when he discusses electric lighting. This same man probably would bore, and be bored, if he were forced to converse about music or Madagascar.

Avoid platitudes and hackneyed phrases. If you meet a friend from a far off place it is not necessary to observe: "How small this world is after all!" "This old world is getting better every day." "It is not so much the high cost of living as the cost of high living." Such observations as these excite about the same degree of admiration as is drawn out by the appearance of a 1903-model touring car. If you have nothing fresh or interesting you can always remain silent. How would you like to read a newspaper that flashed out in bold headlines "Nice Weather We Are Having," or daily gave columns to the same old material you had been reading week after week?

□□□